Central
GLASGOW

G LASGOW is a City of riches. It is rich in its
heritage, rich in its people and, above all, rich
in its Architecture. Much of this, however, became
overlaid with the grime and neglect that followed the
Industrial Revolution and two World Wars concealing,
for a time, the true worth of its buildings.

Latterly, though, it has begun to shake of this
decaying veneer and has emerged to once again
demonstrate its standing as a veritable showcase of
some of the finest buildings in Europe.

All of Scotland salutes this re-emergence and this
excellent guide is a fitting recognition of a stature
regained.

GEORGE B HORSPOOL
PRESIDENT
Glasgow Institute of Architects

© *Authors: Charles McKean, David Walker, Frank Arneil Walker*
Series consultant: David Walker
Cover design: Dorothy Steedman
Picture Research and production: Charles McKean
Editorial Consultant: Duncan McAra

Mainstream Publications (Scotland) Ltd.
Royal Incorporation of Architects in Scotland
ISBN 185158 201 0
1st Published 1989

Cover illustrations:
Front: City centre towers (Douglas Corrance)
Back: Glasgow from the Garden Festival (Charles McKean)

Printed by Macdonald Lindsay Pindar plc, Loanhead, Edinburgh

'A city of wee folk and big windaes' was how the late Jack Coia characterised his city; the accuracy of which anybody studying the immensely statuesque windows in Park Circus or the Victorian suburbs to the west can well appreciate for themselves.

Most Glaswegians characterise or nickname their city according to their personality (from his, it is obvious that Coia was a perceptive, if wee, architect) perhaps because the city lacks the symbol of a pre-eminent physical monument—a Trafalgar Square, an Eiffel Tower or an Edinburgh Castle. Mythologies instead of monuments would have to suffice.

Glaswegian myths tend to be in superlatives: it was either the Second City or the Cancer of the Empire; the workshop of the world, or the workers' republic of Clydeside; it had either the worst slums in Europe, or the best built suburbs in North Britain; its imagery is either that of No Mean City (a city in seemingly terminal decay), or of a city *Miles Better* (in parts, like the curate's egg). It is busy (Glasgow has *always* been busy) becoming the world's first successful post-industrial city, and is determined to earn its laurels as the European City of Culture.

Nothing in Glasgow's history could have presaged its current importance. It had neither royal palace nor fortress; was no capital, nor seat of Government; had neither natural defence, eminence nor harbour. During its life it has faced three catastrophes sufficient to overwhelm a lesser place. The Reformation in 1560 swept away its structure of power and patronage, and with it, much of its ancient economy. American Independence in 1775 decapitated the fabulously wealthy trade with Virginia ruining many of the leading citizens and nearly the city itself. From 1910 onward, the exhaustion of the Lanarkshire ore combined with shifting world trade patterns to leave the city, dangerously dependant upon historic heavy industries, beached and increasingly redundant as the twentieth century progressed.

It has always recovered—painfully, sometimes slowly, and usually metamorphosed. From the ruins of the archbishops rose sturdy 17th century merchants; from the ruin of the Tobacco Lords rose King Cotton; and from the ruins of the shipbuilders?

Given the absence of royal patronage or topographical advantage, the only feature to which one can attribute this extraordinary resilience must be its people: a blend of practical Lowlanders with possibly the greatest concentration of urbanised Celts in the world. The result is a restless, pushy, energetic, rigorous and unsentimental population.

Medieval Glasgow was the fief of bishops and

The name 'Glasgow' was thought to derive from the Gaelic for 'dear green place': an apt description of the elevated, leafy setting at some distance from the Clyde chosen by St Mungo (or Kentigern) for his Cathedral. The current view tends toward an origin equally Gaelic: *glas* for church and *Cun* as an abbreviation for Cunotogernus (or Kentigern). Thus *GlasCun*/Kentigern's Church.

[Glasgow's] powers of recovery have been remarkable and their operation has never been more necessary than the present day... Glasgow trade [is] still struggling to emerge from the largest and most long-continued depression in its history.
Prof Robert Rait 1928

A cold rationalisation of Glasgow's economic position, taking account only of geographical assets, could result in a recommendation to voluntary liquidation, but the same situation has existed more than once in the past and Glasgow men have refused to accept it.... The superb fighting qualities of her citizens— their thrawn individualism—must be turned against her competitors and not against each other
Prof Ronald Miller 1958

OPPOSITE Trinity College photographed by Anne Dick.

INTRODUCTION

Glasgow in 1783.

The Glasgow Square: St Andrew's
Square in 1798.

*The principal merchants, fatigued
with the morning's business, took an
early dinner with their families at
home, and then resorted to the coffee
house or tavern to read the
newspapers, which they generally did
in companies of four or five, over a
bottle of claret or a bowl of punch.*
Alexander 'Jupiter' Carlyle, of the
year 1743

archbishops, inheritors of the church of St Mungo,
to whom King David I granted the jewel amongst his
properties, the manor of Pertheyk (Partick). Around
their hilltop palace and cathedral grew a town, gated
but not entirely walled, populated by grand
ecclesiastics who occupied tall stone houses of a
quantity and quality possibly unrivalled elsewhere in
Scotland. A thriving mercantile community developed
downhill around the Trongate and Stockwellgait.

The Reformation created a power vacuum; and
over the next 130 years, the burgesses of Glasgow
manifested their new power downhill in a new
Tolbooth (1626), St Mary Tron church, the new
College buildings (from 1632), and Hutchesons'
Hospital (1639). After a disastrous fire in 1652, a
rebuilding of the four streets around Glasgow
Cross—Trongate, Gallowgate, High Street,
Saltmarket—created terraces of arcaded tenements
very similar to those surviving in many Italian towns.

The prosperity of the city accelerated with the
growth of the American trade. Glasgow established
industries to supply the American colonies with
staple materials, in return for becoming one of the
principal tobacco ports of Europe. The Tobacco
Lords (as its leaders were known) built themselves
streets of detached Palladian mansions of a type to be
found nowhere else in Britain, exemplified by Miller,
Virginia, Queen and Buchanan Streets. American
Independence annihilated the tobacco trade; but the
industries which had thrived on the back of tobacco,
and the growth of cotton saved the city from disaster.

The Glasgow square, which first appeared in the
late 18th century, is unique to the city. It is a tight,
urban square enclosing a church—as in St Andrew's
Square, St Enoch's Square, and St George's (now
Nelson Mandela) Place—or a prominent civic
building—as in Royal Exchange Square. Altogether
different to the bosky, tree-lined suburban squares of
Edinburgh's New Town or London's West End.

The city's individuality is further emphasised in its
plan. Merchant City streets were designed to be
closed by axially sited prominent buildings, and
comparable street layouts elsewhere in Britain do not
exist.

Heavy industry, consequent upon the discovery and
exploitation of minerals in the immediate hinterland,
transformed Glasgow from a booming cotton town to
the Second City of the Empire. The development of
Blysthwood Hill continued the gridded streets of the
Merchant City, but transformed the plan into an
open-ended street grid more like America than
Britain. It crossed hill and valley with Roman-like
relentlessness. When its inner parts were rebuilt

C McKean

Glasgow from the South c. 1672.

Mitchell Library

Glasgow from the South c. 1761.

Mitchell Library

Glasgow from the South 1868.

upwards after the arrival of mechanical lifts in the late 19th century, the resulting grid-iron canyons of masonry created a townscape redolent of Chicago.

As the eastern suburbs, the south and the riverside became industrial and the High Street a slum—sometimes barely visible beneath the thick black smoke of the St Rollox Works, the wealthy edged west, building streets of honey-coloured mansions over the drumlins of Blythswood Hill, Garnethill, Yorkhill, and Gilmorehill. Thus was Glasgow the Second City of the Empire and the Cancer of the Empire simultaneously—the one the obverse of the other.

At the Lord Provost's (I) had gorgeous State lunch with the Town Council; and was entertained at a great dinner party at night. Unbounded hospitality and enthoozymoozy the order of the day, and I have never been more heartily received anywhere or enjoyed myself so completely. Charles Dickens

5

John Street Church.

An awakening social conscience, public embarrassment, and fear of contagious disease led to action. With the typical lack of sentimentality that distinguishes Glasgow, the ancient heart of the city, was torn down and rebuilt with good clean City Improvement Trust tenements facing new or widened roads.

The later 19th century was characterised by the rebuilding of the central streets—higher and higher after the introduction of the lift—clad in rippling red machine-cut sandstone from the new Dumfriesshire quarries, and enhanced by wondrous figure sculpture. These technical changes provided perfect conditions within which the Glasgow Style in architecture and decoration could flourish.

Central Glasgow was little affected between the Wars. Attention was concentrated, instead, upon expansion of Garden City suburbs like Knightswood, Riddrie, Whitecraigs or Kessington into the countryside. Yet a particularly fine crop of banks, insurance buildings and warehouses, all tall, steel framed and American in derivation, emphasised the transatlantic atmosphere of the city centre.

There has never been anything half hearted about Glasgow. When it determines upon action, there seems to be an underlying impulse to be more thorough, or bigger, or better or more obvious than anywhere else. That it was to have the highest flats in Europe was a matter for civic pride. Given that attitude, we are lucky that anything of the city survived the first post-war flush of enthusiasm. The Bruce Plan proposed a virtual *tabula rasa* of central Glasgow leaving barely an historic stick standing. In 1959, most of Inner Glasgow was put on notice for conversion to a brave new world through the declaration of 29 Comprehensive Development Areas. The Greater Glasgow Transportation Study proposed more motorway miles per head of population than any town in Europe, and the marooning of the Cathedral on a virtual motorway roundabout. The Inner Ring Road was carved through Anderston Cross, Charing Cross, St George's Cross and relegated Cowcaddens to a memory.

For a time, many thought Glasgow would not recover from the resulting thrombosis. That it did, and how it did it, may be inferred from this volume.

Mitchell Library

This guide is an *architectural guide to Glasgow*. The city's evolution and character is nowhere more evident than in its architecture and planning, and from this guide, a reader should be able to understand the history and growth of this great city. From its choice of illustrations, readers should appreciate the fascination to be derived from treading its pavements.

The progenitor of this Guide, although different in format and purpose, is the excellent **Glasgow at a Glance** first published in 1965 and reprinted frequently since. Whereas that is chronological and arranged on a building-by-building basis, this volume is topographical and follows the development of the city, its planning and its townscape as well as individual monuments. Since it also describes many buildings not illustrated (but easily identifiable from the street) it may therefore seem more literary than its predecessor.

There are countless other volumes on the city with which this guide does not intend to compete.

Sequence

The territory covered in this volume is a rough rectangle bounded by Glasgow Cathedral to the north-east, the Botanic Gardens to the north-west, and the Clyde on the south.

It all starts, as did Glasgow, with the Cathedral and ecclesiastical upper town on its hill, extending westwards along Rottenrow to embrace the University of Strathclyde; and genuflects to the ghosts of the Old College and the arcaded mansions of 17th century Glasgow on its way down the High Street. A glimpse east from the Cross along Gallowgate comprehends Calton, Glasgow Green, Charlotte Street, and St Andrew's Square. Clyde Street and the Broomielaw are taken as an entity all the way west to the Kingston Bridge, with all landmarks south of Argyle Street.

Tobacco Lord Glasgow—Trongate, Argyle Street, Candleriggs, Virginia and Miller Streets are taken together, followed by the post-1782 New Town centred upon Ingram and Wilson Streets, ending in George Square and Queen Street. St Vincent Place acts as overture for the heart of Victorian mercantile Glasgow: four great parallel streets streaking uphill north: Buchanan, West Nile, Renfield and Union, and Hope Streets tied together by Gordon Street.

Glasgow from the West c. 1761 a cathedral city of spires and broad streets by a gently flowing river.

Nowadays our leading merchant has too often ceased to be a citizen. Glasgow is the place where he has his office...But he lives as far from it as he can. He cultivates other society. If he has the misfortune to 'speak Glasgow', his sons and his daughters shall escape that 'unmelodious shibolleth', and they come back from their English schools knowing nothing about Glasgow or Glasgow folk.
James Oswald Mitchell 1870.

It is one of the glories of this town that the commoner citizens have a genius for casual friendship...The people of Glasgow—with the exception of those who have sold themselves for a West-end accent—offer you friendship at sight
J R Allan 1938

Looking east down West George Street.

Anne Dick

Blythswood Hill governs the east/west cross streets of Bath, West Regent, West George and St Vincent Street, each taken from their eastern extremity. The principal axis has now moved north from Argyle Street to Sauchiehall Street in the valley between Blythswood and Garnet Hills, Cowcaddens lying on the north slopes of the latter. North Woodside, Park Circus and western Sauchiehall Street, each form a distinct and coherent enclosure enfolding some of the finest urban construction of mid-19th century Europe. Anderston, Yorkhill and Partick take us back to the Clyde and the Kelvin, followed up to Kelvingrove and Gilmorehill. The book ends along Glasgow's third route west, shifting north again from Sauchiehall Street to Great Western Road.

Text Arrangement
Entries for principal buildings follow the sequence of name (or number), address, date and architect (if known). Lesser buildings are contained within paragraphs. Both demolished buildings, (e.g. Old College) and unrealised projects (e.g. the University on Woodside Hill) are included if appropriate. In general the dates given are those of the design (if known) or of the beginning of construction (if not). Text in the small column is illustrative of less architectural aspects of the city.

Map References
The map to be found on the back end paper gives diagrammatic coverage of the area of the Guide. The numbers do not refer to page numbers—rather to references in the text itself. Where there is a great number of buildings in the same street (e.g. Buchanan Street) space has allowed only few numbers, sufficient for visitors to take bearings.

Authors' Note
In our preparations, we have been much assisted by the trenchant comments and knowledge of the contemporary scene of Archie Doak, co-editor of **Glasgow at a Glance**. Neil Baxter assisted in the initial stages of preparation of the university area.

The high level of illustration, and the colour illustrations in particular, would have been utterly impossible at the current price without the financial and enthusiastic support of Glasgow District Council and the Scottish Development Agency.

Whereas every effort has been made to achieve total accuracy, the authors would welcome any corrigenda. Many people, listed in the acknowledgements on page 200-1, have assisted them in the preparation, but the responsibility for any inaccuracies must remain the authors'.

I have often been asked, and that too in very far away parts of the world, as to where I was born. My answer at times has been that I was 'Clyde-built'. The metaphor was scarcely ever misunderstood
William 'Crimean' Simpson 1899

Glasgow Cathedral painted by Charles Rennie Mackintosh.

The Cathedral, the Upper Town and the University. *Left above* the Cathedral and the Molendinar Burn painted at the turn of the 18th/19th century by H W Williams. *Left* the Blacader Aisle.

Top the Archbishop's Palace and Glasgow Cathedral painted by Thomas Hearne, c. 1782. *Above* the Provand's Lordship and its original neighbours in the new Upper Town, painted in the 1820s by William Simpson. Simpson notes in the margin that Glasgow's hangman used to live in a single storey cottage on the left. *Top right* Fiddler's Close, off the High Street painted by William Simpson. *Centre right* the Lion and Unicorn Staircase, painted by Thomas Fairbairn. *Right* the Hunterian Museum, Old College, by William Stark (drawn by William Playfair).

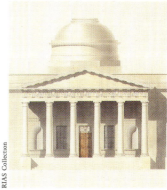

Top William Simpson's painting of Glasgow High Street and the University in the 1830s. Note the Professors' lodgings on the right and Tolbooth Steeple in the distance. *Above* Glasgow Cathedral from near the Wellgate, c. 1840. Painter unknown.

1 **Glasgow Cathedral**, principally 13th century, is of truly European grandeur, dug deep into the hillside of the Molendinar Burn. The slope provided the opportunity for a double choir, one below the other. Although traces of Bishop Jocelyn's earlier church can be seen in the Laigh Kirk, the design is predominantly that of the early 13th century which the nave, although completed a century later, still honoured. (Colour plate, p. 9)

Glasgow Cathedral with Archbishop's Palace and the Upper Town; Old College towers on the left. Drawn, probably in 1672, by Captain John Slezer. The Cathedral retains its two western towers, removed in the 19th century in the pursuit of symmetry.

The **Laigh Kirk** is a veritable forest of stocky columns and sturdy vaulting, with a curious Gothic canopy around St Mungo's shrine, embellished with superb stiff-leaf carvings on the capitals. The hushed chapels at the east end, at the lower level by the Chapter House and the well, offer total isolation from the city outside. From the Reformation until the late 18th century, the Laigh Kirk formed the Barony Kirk, in which Sir Walter Scott set the first meeting of Frank Osbaldistone and Rob Roy: *'Conceive an extensive range of low-browed, dark and twilight vaults such as are used for sepulchres in other countries...and had long been dedicated to the same purpose in this, a portion of which was seated with pews and used as a church.'* The white marks on the columns date from its use as a burial ground once the Barony congregation left for its new premises.

Section through Glasgow Cathedral's east end, drawn by James Collie.

The **Blacader Aisle**, from the turn of the 15th/16th centuries, occupies a skin contemporary with the 13th-century Choir. The exquisite vaulting built by Archbishop Blacader is glowing white, offering the brightest part of the Cathedral. (Colour plate, p. 10)

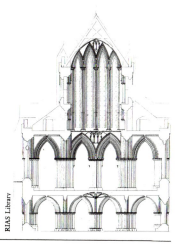

RIAS Library

C

RCAHMS

RIAS Collection

RIAS Collection

RIAS Library

Top right Choir and nave. *Top* the Lady Chapel. *Middle* the Laigh Kirk. *Above* Stairs down to the Laigh Kirk drawn by James Collie.

The architectural effect of the **Church** is achieved by proportion and simplicity. Although small by European standards, it seems immense by virtue of the narrowness in relation to height of the choir and nave; accentuated by the shallowness of the transepts which end flush with the aisle walls. The building is squeezed upwards and all the details accentuate that—little carving, but depth of detail and massing: *'nane o' yere whigmaleeries and curliewurlies and open-steek hems about it—a' solid, weel-jointed masonwark, that will stand as lang as the warld, keep hands and gunpother aff it'* (thus Andrew Fairservice speaking for Walter Scott in *Rob Roy*).

Note particularly the timber vaulting of the Choir, the arcades of the Lady Chapel, the square Chapter House and the vaulted Sacristy above. The **Crossing** is magnificent: tall, slender transepts, the depth only of the aisles, light a space busy with movement and detail. A beautiful 15th-century rood screen with cusped parapet and carved figures frames the stairs up into the Choir; stairs descend on either side down into the Laigh Kirk, and the glowing tomb of the Blacader Aisle on the south. The windows of the north transept and the lancets of the great east gable are arrows pointing to the sky.

Splendid wall-tombs in the kirkyard.

Open to the public: guidebook available

C McKean

RIAS Library

RCAHMS

2 **Necropolis**, from 1833, John Bryce
Competition-winning design to transform the
Merchants' Fir Park pleasure grounds to a graveyard
inspired by the celebrated Père Lachaise in Paris.
The dream of Dr John Strang, the now somewhat
desolate mound is swathed with paths which meander
through a wealth (in every meaning of that word) of
carved tributes to the dead and dread. There are
catacombs, an enclosure for Jews, Egyptian vaults,
and a fascinating collection of highly crafted minor
works by some of Glasgow's best architects including

Top the Rood Screen and Crossing,
drawn by Railton. *Above* the Minto
Monument. *Left* the proposed
restoration of the Cathedral by George
Meikle Kemp, architect of the Scott
Monument, Edinburgh.

NECROPOLIS

A garden cemetery, as Dr John Strang described his idea, would be *not only beneficial to public morals, to the improvement of manners, but likewise calculated to extend virtuous and generous feelings...A garden cemetery is the sworn foe to preternatural fear and superstition...It was from the gloomy, naked and deserted cemetery that superstition drew her chief influence...Adorn the sepulchre, and the frightful visions which visit the midnight pillow will disappear...A garden cemetery and monumental decoration afford the most convincing tokens of a nation's progress in civilization and in the arts which are its result...*

Monuments in the Necropolis: *Above left* Buchanan of Dowanhill (1844, James Brown). *Above right* Robert Minter monument (1844, John Stephen), Knox monument. *Right* Bridge of Sighs. *Below* Ruchill Mausoleum.

John Baird (see Blythswood Square, p. 117), John Bryce, Alexander Thomson, Charles Wilson (see Park Circus, p. 166), and—perhaps above all—J T Rochead. The architecture swings from Egyptian catacomb, through Gothic (Wilson's odd Montgomerie Monument), Greek (three versions of that architect's totem, the monument Lysicrates erected in Athens upon winning a choral competition—hence *choragic monument*), Romanesque to florid. The contemporary **Bridge of Sighs** over the Molendinar Burn (now sadly culverted beneath Wishart Street) was designed by David and James Hamilton, as were the Gates in 1838 and the Lodge, in 1839. Thomas Hamilton provided the 1825 monument to **John Knox**, David Cousin the miniature Templars' Church of the **Menteith Mausoleum** in 1842, J T Rochead the Greek Doric temple of the **Ruchill Mausoleum** of 1851 (curious in the light of Rochead's later, furious Scottishness) and J A Bell the Moorish kiosk monument to the explorer **Rae Wilson**, 1849. **Open to the public: leaflet available**

Mitchell Library

The Upper Town

The medieval upper town consisted of manses and houses for Cathedral dignitaries, many built in response to Bishop Cameron's instruction to his 32 parsons to build in the four streets adjoining the Cathedral in the early 15th century. There were some charitable foundations, noblemen's town houses, and the purpose-built Vicars' Alley just to the north of the Cathedral. Of these, only one survives.

The once limpid **Molendinar Burn** ran in a ravine by the eastern edge of the Cathedral, down behind the University Gardens, westwards just south of Gallowgate, and south to the Green, west of St Andrew's Square, by St Andrew's by the Green. The Latin origins of its name confirm its early use as power for mills. By the mid 19th century it had become little more than an animal-befouled sewer, and was culverted by the City Improvement Trust after 1865. The City's increasing cleanliness could permit the Molendinar's re-opening.

Archbishop's Palace

A 'great tower' was added, c.1436, by Bishop John Cameron (Chancellor of the Realm) to a considerable pre-existing castle that occupied a huge triangular site before the gates of the Cathedral. In 1510 Archbishop Beaton built an *exceeding high wall of hewen stone* and corner tower and, in 1544, Archbishop Gavin Dunbar contributed a massive, twin-towered gatehouse. The great tower was already ruinous when used for Jacobite prisoners in 1715, and all remnants were finally removed in 1789. (Colour plate, p. 11)

Above Glasgow from the east, drawn by Robert Paul in the mid 18th century. It shows the upper town including Drygate, the Archbishop's Palace, and the Duke's Lodging with its gazebo. *Below* the Duke's Lodging in the 19th century.

C McKean

The Duke's Lodging, possibly the grandest nobleman's house in old Glasgow, was created from the Manse of the Rector of Eaglesham, which fell to the Stuarts of Minto in 1586, who sold it to the Graham family of nearby Mugdock in 1605. The Grahams began to transform it into an arcaded, courtyard mansion with gardens and gazebo, nicknamed, after the aggrandisement of the Grahams to the Dukedom of Montrose, the **Duke's Lodging** (hence Duke Street).

The High Street, with Robert Adam's Infirmary soaring above, drawn by J C Nattes, 1798.

Nattes/McKean

Provand's Lordship was built as the Manse for the adjacent St Nicholas Hospital, founded by Bishop de Durisdere for 'a priest and twelve old men' in 1464. It also housed the Prebend of Balornock or Provan from which it derives its current name. In the 19th century it was more generally known as the 'Black Land'. Within its substantial and impressive rooms are majestic pieces of ancient furniture, and the People's Palace collection of paintings by William Simpson. **Open to the public. Leaflet available**.

Martyrs' School.

Assist

Townhead

The glory of the upper town vanished after the Reformation. The Town's Trades occupied the Parsonage of Morebattle in the High Street and the other manses survived as shelter for mechanics or the poor. The setting remained sufficiently idyllic for the domed **Infirmary** by Robert and James Adam to be located here in 1792. It provided eight wards each with 17 beds, and was distinguished by a pedimented portico of Corinthian columns. The arrival of the Bridewell (and then the Duke Street Gaol), factories, tenements, gasworks and—above all—the exceptionally noisome St Rollox chemical works, piled indignity upon indignity. Ancient buildings were replaced by densely built tenements of the poorer sort, schools and churches intermingled with factories; and then by new roads. It was only by a near-miss that the Cathedral avoided being marooned upon a traffic island.

3 **Provand's Lordship**, 1471; rear, later Steep-roofed, corbie-gabled, three-storeyed stone manse with dormer windows and armorial panels typical of the dwellings of Glasgow's great ecclesiastics. Shortened, shorn of its original chimney stacks, dormer windows and somehow diminished by its lowered roof, it remains nonetheless large and imposing for a non-aristocratic Scots medieval town house. (Colour plate, p. 11)

Martyrs' School, 1895, Charles Rennie Mackintosh Named after Covenanters James Lawson, James Nisbet and Alexander Wood, executed on this spot (known as the Howgatehead) in 1684. A T-plan, red sandstone box converted by ASSIST Architects into a performing arts centre: Mackintosh quality particularly visible in the doors, stairwells and great roof trusses. **St Mungo's RC Church**, Parson Street,

Page and Park

was designed by George Goldie, 1869-71, whilst the
red stone Gothic of the nearby **Retreat** followed 20
years later by Fr Osmund Cooke.

Glasgow Infirmary, 1904-14, James Miller
On the site of Robert Adam's Infirmary, to which its
south-facing domed façade is a heavy handed-tribute,
neither this design, nor Miller, was the first chosen.
Miller's snatch of the commission from the
competition-winner H E Clifford left ill will in
Glasgow. The horizontality of the modern Infirmary
betrays the hand of Sir Basil Spence, Glover &
Ferguson, whose long programme was completed in
1981. The **Dispensary** (originally the Blind Asylum)
received its distinctive tower from William Landless
in 1879. A clean would reveal its spark and the
sculpture of Christ restoring the sight of the blind by
Charles Grassby.

William III Statue, 1735,
possibly Peter Scheemakers
Celebrated bronze relocated from its original site
facing the Tontine Rooms in Trongate. Its tail is
reputed to be attached by a ball-joint so that it can
switch in the wind.

Halls of Residence, MacLeod Street, 1985,
G R M Kennedy & Partners
Red-brick blocks of student residences attempting to
enclose the street with something like tenement scale,
echoes of Mackintosh's Scotland Street School
staircases used as punctuation marks. The residence
becomes emboldened as it proceeds westward and

Cathedral Square and the Friends' Visitors' Centre.

The construction of the
competition-winning **Cathedral
Square** by Page & Park, and of
the new **Friends' Visitors Centre**
by Ian Begg (with Page & Park),
presents the chance for the creation
of an enclave around the Cathedral
which is a reasonable 20th-century
version of what it might have been
in the 16th. In the right weather
once dark has fallen, the ancient
mysteriousness of this spot reasserts
itself. It is still the heart of
Glasgow, and may become so again
as the University of Strathclyde
returns to colonise those streets
abandoned by the University of
Glasgow so long ago.

G R M Kennedy

Right the Barony Church, now being converted into a ceremonial hall for Strathclyde University. *Above* Forbes Hall.

Barony North Church.

C McKean

along Cathedral Street, into the brick campus of **Forbes Hall**: corner towers, dormer windows, much red brick, Post-Modern arched pends and, at the centre, the **Lord Todd**, a virulent scarlet brick bar with Toshery overtones.

Barony Church, 1 Castle Street, 1886-90, Sir J J Burnet and John A Campbell
The first church outside the Cathedral Laigh Kirk was a remarkably ugly 1798 invention by James Adam and John Robertson in illiterate baronial. Its competition-winning successor is of a staggering Gothic thoroughness. Early English in period, and Scottish in proportion and detail, it resembles Dunblane Cathedral outside, and Glasgow Cathedral within, executed in warm red sandstone. Its incumbent in 1929, the Rev John White, was the prime mover in the unification of the Church of Scotland.

4 **Barony North Church**, 1878, John Honeyman
A graceful white Italianate intruder into this primeval domain: each Corinthian column topped by a statue rising above the balustrade. A pleasant pilastered belfry at the west end, and a gallery on cast-iron columns within. Its sophistication is enhanced by the dark, baronial cragginess of **Cathedral House**, its only surviving neighbour, designed by Campbell Douglas & Morrison in 1896 for discharged prisoners.

Rottenrow
The most significant feature about the upper town is its height, high on a ridge above Glasgow; subject to wind and blessed with superb views for those who quit their cars. Along that ridge ran Rottenrow, formerly the principal route west out of

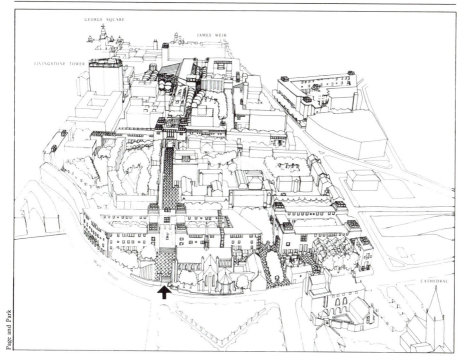

Page and Park

Glasgow, through a fortified Gate where now stands the pleasant Dutch-gabled, stone **Balmanno Centre**. The red sandstone tenements are indifferently crowstepped, although well cleaned, and the grey stone 1885 **Board School** at the corner of Collins Street by Baldie & Tennant is majestic of its type. A campus scheme for Strathclyde University by Page & Park proposes the promotion of Rottenrow to a principal processional route.

Aerial drawing of Strathclyde University campus by Page & Park. Cathedral and the Visitors' Centre are right foreground, and the Barony Kirk centre, at the entrance to Rottenrow as a new processional route leading up to the School of Architecture.

5 **University of Strathclyde**
Landscaping and sculptural henges fail to modify the essentially utilitarian nature of the campus of this business-like University: probably an adequate commentary upon the original aesthetic aspirations of technocrats. Although a competition has just been held for its transformation into something more colourful and contemporary, no results can yet be perceived. The campus dominates the Rottenrow ridge down both sides. The New Town streets, built uphill c.1802 into what was then Deanside Brae, North Portland Street, Richmond Street etc, have fallen prey to carbuncular university departments, and all that remains of Upper Montrose Street is the red baroque flank of the Royal Technical College, immediate parent of Strathclyde University. The **School of Architecture**, 1966, by Frank Fielden &

The Colville Building; the School of Architecture on the left.

RMJM

21

The Tech, as it was known—or the Royal College of Science and Technology (to give it its title)—was founded in 1795 by Professor John Anderson, with the name the Andersonian Institution. Its first Professors were the curious Dr Thomas Garnett, who left one of the most interesting records of contemporary Scotland in his **Tour** published in 1802, and after whose Observatory Garnethill takes its name; and Professor Birkbeck (later of Birkbeck College in London). Birkbeck left the following record: '*I beheld, in these unwashed artificers, the evident sign of the sacred flame of science. I could not refrain from asking myself "Why should poverty prevent these minds from acquiring that knowledge of which they are so eagerly in quest? Why should that poverty close to them the avenues of science?"*' Anderson's legacy provided the means, and the result became Glasgow's second university. The College was first housed in a building originally erected for Glasgow's ancient Grammar School in 1780, facing George Street: a classical, ashlar-fronted building with a pedimented porch, the Hall's dome behind, good mouldings and a balustrade. It contained a library, laboratories, committee rooms and a spherical hall seating 500 (see p. 78).

Right Central College of Commerce. *Below* Clydesdale Bank, Cathedral Street.

Associates, is good of its Brutalist type with spacious but spartan interiors rejoicing in raw materials in their natural state, and the **Business School** was designed by G R M Kennedy. The strongly horizontal, white-tiled **Colville Building** was designed in 1968 by Robert Matthew Johnston-Marshall & Partners on the same podium level as the School of Architecture. All is mugged by the ruddy-hued **Livingstone Tower**, 1963, by Covell Matthews.

Clydesdale Bank, Cathedral Street, 1980, Mackay & Forrester
Plainly elegant brick cube, capped by a dominant pavilion-roof with cut-away corner windows. **Allan Glen's School** is a graceful example of the well-proportioned geometric glass schools of the 1960s. At its western end, Cathedral Street preserved a small remnant of its former enclosure with **St Andrew's Free Church** (now a furniture store), 1843, by J T Rochead, in dignified, white plasterer's Gothic. The red corner tower of the 1895 **Apostolic Church** by Colin Menzies is chunky turn-of-the-century Renaissance.

Wylie Shanks

6 **Central College of Commerce**, 300 Cathedral Street, 1963, Wylie Shanks
Elegantly black and white, horizontally proportioned block, transformed by the sculptural, neo-Corbusian structures on its roof. The following year the same architects designed the more subtle **Glasgow Colleges of Building and Printing** virtually across the road. Dramatic sculptural shapes adorn the roof, and the slab is subtly enhanced by the slight bend in the façade, and by the contrast between solid white gable and the dark glass curtain walls.

McKay and Forrester

Ladywell Housing, 1964, Honeyman Jack & Robertson

A breezy mixture of tall towers and lower blocks characteristic of the better housing of the period. The openness of its layout was in deliberate contrast to the grimness of the Duke Street Gaol which it replaced. The 1901 red sandstone **Bell of the Brae** tenements by Burnet & Boston, sprightly after their wash, were competition-winners in 1901: a steep, curving crowstepped sweep downhill toward the Merchant City and round into the first stages of Duke Street.

Duke Street was proposed in 1764 by the Carron Company of Falkirk as a more direct route from the city through Cumbernauld to Carron. It was named after the **Duke's Lodging** which had edged the junction of Drygate and the route east since late medieval times. The enormous classical hulk of **Great Eastern Hotel**, with quoins, rusticated ground floor, wings and pedimented windows, was designed as Alexander's cotton spinning mill by Charles Wilson in 1848-9. Its classical clothes conceal a cast-iron, fireproof frame of arched floors of concrete over bent corrugated iron sheeting. Converted to an hotel by Neil Duff in 1909. The main block of the 1858 **Ladywell School** by John Burnet sen (funded by James Alexander of the adjacent mill), consists of an Ionic-columned arcade, with an improving literary sculptured head (eg

Wylie Shanks

Above Glasgow Colleges of Building and Printing.

Left Glasgow's finest remaining mill: now the Great Eastern Hotel. Note Ladywell School tower in the distance.

Anne Dick

Right Kirkhaven. *Below* arcaded buildings of Glasgow's High Street which survived to Victorian times.

RCAHMS

Glasgow's arcaded streets derived from Council regulations to ensure that there would be no inflammable timber projections: *Each person building de novo on the Hie Street, or repairing, sall be obleiged and is hereby obleist to doe it by stonework from heid to foot, back and foir, without any timber or daill except in the insett thereof, which is understood to be partitions, door, windoes, presses and such lyk...not only for their probable security but also for the decoring of the said Burgh...to build the same with stone, except the Toun Counsell licence them, quhilk they will tak into their consideratioune how far they may without spoyling the broadness of the streit, they always repairing it with stone in the foir work, by arched pillars, and by how many as the Toun Counsell, by the advyce of architectors, sall think most convenient.* Stone arcades thus propped up stone buildings jettied out over the public pavement underneath—so narrow that you could '*not walk therein with any conveniency*'. They offered vaulted ground-floor storage cellars for '*merchants who came to attend the fairs to stow their goods in at night*'. The land remained the property of the Council until 1801, when it decided to sell the land behind the arcades for shops at £5 per square yard.

Shakespeare) above each column. Note the attenuated leaning tower. The grandiose **Kirkhaven**, 1857, by Peddie & Kinnear, is one of Glasgow's superb pagan temples for Presbyterians, who rejected the ritualistic overtones of Gothic in favour of an austere late classicism—in this case Grecian. **Wellpark School**, immediately behind, is plainly Italianate with

Mitchell Library

underscaled pedimented pavilions on each corner and a domed cupola that seems unrelated to the rest. No urban character beyond, until Duke Street can be seen entering the close-knit Victorian suburb of Dennistoun (outside this volume's compass).

High Street

Glasgow's 17th-century growth in mercantile self-confidence was expressed downhill: a new Tolbooth in 1626, a new University façade, the new Hutchesons' Hospital on the Trongate in 1639, a new Grammar School (near Ingram Street) and a Merchants' Hall in the Briggait surrounded by fine stone, Netherlandish town houses in the Briggait, Stockwell and Saltmarket. A grievous fire on 17 June 1652 burnt out most of the old timber buildings then facing the principal streets, gutting a large area as far north as Bell Street, most of the Gallowgate, Trongate and the Saltmarket: some eighty closes in all. A second fire in 1677 destroyed over 130 houses more.

The rebuilding created, according to Daniel Defoe, *'the four principal streets...the fairest for breadth and the finest built that I have ever seen. The lower storeys, for the most part, stand on vast, square Doric columns with arches which open into the shops—adding to the strength as well as to the beauty of the buildings. In a word, 'tis one of the cleanliest, most beautiful, and best built cities in Great Britain'.*

The Bell of the Brae (ie summit) was recorded by Blind Harry as being the location of a battle between Sir William Wallace and his opponents c.1300, when the area to the south was still open country. No other record of this skirmish survives. The upper part of the High Street was very steep and dangerous (which may acount for the initial isolation of the upper town after the Reformation) until 20 ft was sliced off the top in 1772 to render access to the Cathedral easier for church goers, more in 1783, and a further decapitation some decades later. The High Street narrowly missed being utterly flattened and straightened in the improvements of 1800 to align with the grid of the New Town.

Left Glasgow's High Street in 1834 drawn by John Scott shows striking similarities to Edinburgh's High Street. Note the University tower peeping above the chimneys.

By 1853, the High Street had become 'squalid and repulsive' according to Hugh MacDonald: *'Sin and misery are indeed here to be seen in loathsome union. Strange glimpses of the City's hidden life are obtained as we pass the noisome vennels. Squalid mothers are peeping from closes with wan and filthy children whom it is a pain to look upon... higher and higher we ascend leaving Drygate Street and Rottenrow with their antique edifices disappearing fast in the march of civic improvement..we now pursue our way in an eastern direction... the great city dims the autumn sky with its canopy of smoke...the pestiferous smoke from certain works in the northern quarter of the city, notwithstanding their gigantic chimneys, seems to have thrown a blight over the face of nature. The trees are for the most part shrivelled'*

The COLLEDGE of GLASGOW

Slezer/McKean

GLASGOW
OLD COLLEGE.

RIAS Library

Mitchell Library

RCAHMS

Swan/McKean

Top the Old College in 1672. *Middle* the main courtyard in 1761. *Above* College Gardens in 1832. *Left* William Adam's 1732 Library. *Middle left* Old College entrance drawn by A McGibbon.

Old College, from 1630, John Boyd, mason,
followed by John Clerk
A magnificent example of the distinctive school of
Scots masoncraft which developed as the Scottish
Renaissance. Two large, interlinked courts were
joined through a pend above which soared the
University tower with its characteristic Dutch
steeple. Of its magnificent façade, some survives in
Pearce Lodge, Gilmorehill (see p. 185). Internal
fittings from the Fore Hall can be found in the new
Senate Room, and the 1690 Lion and Unicorn
staircase, which led up to it from the Outer Court, is
rebuilt against the west wing. Seven acres of pleasure
grounds sloped down to the Molendinar, to which
were added over the next 150 years, an
Observatory, an **Examination Hall**, 1811, by
Peter Nicholson, the **Library** , 1732, a pretty little
temple designed by William Adam, and most
notably, William Stark's 1804 majestic Doric pavilion
for the **Hunterian Museum**.
(Colour plates, p. 11)

Glasgow University
Founded in 1451 by Bishop
William Turnbull, the University
first met in the Blackfriars Kirk,
and thereafter in the Cathedral
itself, its Chancellor being the
(Arch) bishop. In 1460, Lord
James Hamilton endowed it with
lands adjacent to the Blackfriars in
the High Street, and the Faculty of
Arts soon abandoned the **Auld
Pedagoguy** in Rottenrow for the
concentration of University
properties in the High Street. The
Reformation caused such a seizure
that the University ceased to
operate for three years, and was
rescued by Queen Mary in 1560
with the gift of the lands of the
Blackfriars and Greyfriars in the
High Street. In the 1630s, the
University determined to rebuild
the properties which it owned in
the High Street, utilising the half-
built **Pedagoguy**; at least the
north wing of the Inner Court had
been completed by 1632, and the
principal High Street façade
followed in 1639.

RCAHMS

Professors' Lodgings, James Adam, 1793
(demolished)
Imperial style blocks flanking a proposed vista down
College Street designed by John Jaffrey, to a new
Corn Market by the Adams. Only the Professors'
Lodgings, used for a time to house the Hunterian,
were built.

British Linen Bank, 215 High Street, 1895,
W Forrest Salmon
Rare survivor on the west side: vertiginous red
sandstone façade with Renaissance details, a cupola
on the skyline. Strathclyde University plans a new
complex on the George Street/Shuttle Street site by
Benson & Forsyth. Urban scale reappears further
south with the grandiose 1891 tenement at **Nos**

Left James Adam's proposal for
Professors' Lodgings closing a vista
down Shuttle Street to a new Corn
Market. *Below* John Jaffrey's design for
Shuttle Street itself.

University of Glasgow

Above Babbity Bowster's. *Right* James Adam's designs for Stirling Square.

97-101 at the corner of Blackfriars Street, with its Corinthian pilasters, by A B MacDonald.

8 **Babbity Bowster's**, Blackfriars Street, 1792, James Adam
Sole survivor of Stirling's Street and Square planned by John Stirling, in 1792, on the large plot of land behind his family's High Street tenement. He commissioned James Adam, who designed shop and warehouse premises at the ground floor within a large palace frontage. Unfortunately, Stirling *'failed in acquiring some property essential to his plan, and therefore formed the present confused Square or Place'*. This *'queer, out of the way place, a sort of aneurism on South Albion Street'* was largely destroyed by the Improvement Trust and all that survives is the curious **Babbity Bowster's** bistro, recreated in 1986 by Nicholas Groves-Raines. The early 20th-century red stone warehouse adjacent is smartly dressed in 18th-century classical blind-arched windows and roundels.

Gas Workshops, Blackfriars Street, from 1878
Renaissance-fronted building opposite Bowster's (becoming Italianate as it runs down Walls Street), converted into a fine courtyard of flats.

17th-century Fiddler's Close, possibly the most picturesque of the timber closes which survived the fires, lay just opposite Babbity Bowster's. Before its descent into slumdom, it was the *'Buchanan Street of Georgian Glasgow'* as a Victorian commentator put it, and home of some of Glasgow's most fashionable shops, as the following 1780 advertisement recalls: *'Just arrived at Kirkland's. Fiddler's Closs, Langley's rich and elegant assortment, of India, London and Manchester'*. It was replaced by the Gas Showroom in 1878. (Colour plate, p. 11). *'The portion of the City from the Cross northward has, for a quarter of a century, been notorious for its overcrowding, and it has been distinguished as being the principal rendezvous of the scum and the blackguards of the city...A few months ago, the whole of the tenements in Fiddler's Close were ordered to be taken down. Some have accordingly been removed, and wagon loads of thatch have recently been carried from this locality to some cowfeeder's premises, there to be converted into manure.*

C McKean

Above Bell Street warehouses.

Bell Street

The first post-medieval street in Glasgow: now a dramatic tunnel penetrating to the heart of the Merchant City. Buildings lining the north side between the High Street and Walls Street are white and Italianate, by John Carrick & M S MacDonald, 1890, and Burnet Boston & Carruthers, 1903. **No 51**, by A B MacDonald, 1902, fronted a market behind. Tall, red City Improvement Trust warehouses, offices and shops by Thomson & Sandilands, 1910, line the south side. **Nos 6-20** were erected during the First World War by Campbell Reid & Wingate, in the large, red, steel-framed manner to become customary after 1918.

Bell Street looking west.

9 **Railway Warehouses**, Bell Street, 1882-3 Gigantic, curving, Piranesi-like edifice in the form of an Italian Renaissance palazzo—extruded in every direction, stripped of superfluity, reinforced with mass-concrete arched floors. Recently converted into flats by James Cunning, Young & Partners.

The warehouse at **No 118-126**, c.1880, shares a common rectangularity with those in adjacent **Watson Street**, 1880, their treatment of solid and void, their Greek key incised carving, their giant pilasters superimposed upon subsidiary ones, almost certainly posthumous to Alexander Thomson.

C McKean

GALLOWGATE

Gallowgate looking west to the Tolbooth Steeple, in 1834.

Scott/McKean

'**On the arrival** *of the mail at the Saracen's Head, all the idlers of the city crowded around it and at the door stood two waiters "who were specially selected for their handsome appearance" with embroidered coats, red plush breeches, and powdered hair. When the Judges, or the sporting Duke of Hamilton were expected, the waiters got themselves up in still more ornate style, and even mounted silk stockings. On these occasions, they were looked up to with awe, wonder and respect by all the urchins of the neighborhood.'*

Gallowgate

Most travellers entered the city along Gallowgate, and the city proper began at the Gallowgate Port (removed in 1749) where Barrack Street branches off. Its location at the nearest point of contact to London and Edinburgh made it a focus for transport, carriages, mails and—therefore—of the great inns. The best known was the **Saracen's Head** built by Robert Tennant in 1754 of 'good, hewen stone' robbed from the Castle, on the site of Little St Mungo's Chapel. Here stayed Dr Johnson and James Boswell on their visit in 1769. From the mid 18th century, the Gallowgate became the centre for dyeworks, potteries, tanneries, breweries, and other noxious industries (particularly the cudbear factory making dyes from moss) and from then on, the Gallowgate was lost.

It retains none of the formality of a central Glasgow street. Rather it is clearly the place where people are making the most of their opportunity. The very buildings seem to move in sympathy with the vast energy being expended in this warren of embryonic business. The recently cleaned **Dovehill Court** recalls the Andersons of Dowhill, or Dovehill, one of the most important Glasgow dynasties in the 17/18th centuries; and the fine, patterned brick former Saracen Tool Works, 1896, by Honeyman & Keppie still clings to Great Dovehill.

Mission Building, East Campbell Street, 1863 Haig & Low
Recent cleaning has revealed the fine stone pilasters and Grecian anthemion-leafed carvings of these followers of Charles Wilson.

Claythorn Street, 1771
The two buildings flanking Claythorn Street on Gallowgate, at the outer edge of the old City, were

One of the two 1771 houses flanking the entrance to Claythorn Street.

Anne Dick

built as houses and inns. That to the east, with its
fine wallhead gable, quoins, turnpike stair and
scrolled skewputts, has been restored as part of a new
red brick sheltered housing development by SSHA
architects; **Highland Jessie's** to the west, by
McGurn Logan Duncan Opfer. The **Royal Bank**,
471 Gallowgate, is a smart, classical 1930s bank by
Eric Sutherland, flanking John Carrick's 1875
processional archway to the Markets—a fine pediment
on paired Doric columns. Impressive cast-iron
market-halls within.

The Barras

Graced with its upmarket, SDA-approved English
nomenclature 'Barrowland', this celebrated flea
market occupies most of the territory between
Gallowgate and London Road from Ross Street to
Bain Street, its principal entrances newly dignified
with lacy, cast-iron gateways. It is otherwise a
mixture of buildings of all ages—tenements, sheds,
warehouses, pavements, and the 50s dance hall.

Above Entrance to the markets. *Left* Clay Pipe Factory, Bain Street.

10 **Clay Pipe Factory**, Bain Street, 1876,
Matthew Forsyth
Distinctive red and white brick façades flank one
entrance to the Barras: in stone, they would have
been unremarkable amidst contemporary St Vincent
Street. In striated brick, they are truly amazing.
Facing them across a newly landscaped Square, and
making a small amount of sense in this blitzed area,

The Barras

Most Glaswegians presume that the
name 'Barras' is a corruption of
'the barrows' named after the
weekend flea-market. There are two
more likely origins. The lands
occupied by 'ra Barras' were
previously known as 'Barrowflats'
an ancient patrimony whose origins
date back at least to the
Reformation. A more likely source
is the name of the gate at the foot
of the Saltmarket—the **Barras
Port**: the name a corruption either
from 'the Burgh's (Barras) Port' or
from the French 'barré'.

Calton

The old weaving village of Calton
was feued by the Barrowfield estate
in 1705 and came to occupy a large
area between the Gallowgate and
Glasgow Green beyond the city
boundary. By 1798, it had become
'very populous (with) many streets,
which are in general built of brick
and covered with tile'. The place of
early religious riots, dangerous
radicals and of Trade Union riots,
where genteel people never
ventured, it thrived just outside the
control of the City's Guilds, and
was thus the place of refuge for
fugitives from Glasgow: Scotland's
equivalent of London's notorious
Alsatia.

In Old Calton Graveyard is the following badly eroded memorial stone: *This is the property of the WEAVING BODY under charge of the five districts of Calton. Erected to the memory of John Page, Alexander Miller and James Ainsley who at a meeting of that Body for resisting a reduction of their wages were upon the 2nd Sep 1787 Martyred by the Military under orders of the Civic Authority of Glasgow firing upon the Multitude. Also to the Memory of the...in trade...James Granger interred at...James Gray, Alexander Megget, Duncan Cherry, James Morton, Thomas Miller, John Jaffrey.*

Above Calton Police Station. Below Templeton's Carpet Factory.

is the 1836 **Calton New Parish Church**, spruced up and brightly rendered: a box kirk with an Italianate pilastered and pedimented front.

Police Station, Tobago Street, 1868, John Carrick
A dignified two-storeyed, seven-bay classical building with architraved windows, quoins and a channelled stonework plinth.

London Road
John Weir's elegantly classical London Street was smashed into the Saltmarket in the 1820s, and joined Great Hamilton and Canning Streets to form London Road. At one time lined with good buildings, particularly as it passed the Green back to back with Monteith Row, little is now left. **St Alphonsus'**, a late work by Peter Paul Pugin, c.1905, is typically muscular, in somewhat unlovable red rubble Gothic with traceried windows.

11 **People's Palace**, 1894, A B MacDonald
Red sandstone institutional with delightful Winter Gardens at the rear. It contains the People's History of Glasgow—the Tobacco Lords, the Calton Weavers, reconstructions of Victorian bathrooms, tenements, shops and single ends. They come to admire Billy Connolly's banana boots. The collection (cramped like someone's attic) offers the pleasure and pain of accidental recognition of items you thought commonplace now displayed as history.

McLennan Arch, 1796, James Adam
The central bay from the principal floor of Adam's Athenaeum in Ingram Street retrieved after demolition. That this gigantic triumphal arch once sat above a full-storey height plinth gives a powerful indication of the grandiose scale of the piano nobile of the Athenaeum.

12 **Templeton's Carpet Factory (Doge's Palace)**, 1889, William Leiper
One of the most extravagant polychromatic brick buildings in Britain, broadcasting an international outlook and cosmopolitan taste, Venetian in style, with details far more various and inventive than its nickname implies. Its construction was damaged by an architect/engineer dispute, the engineer refusing to tie the façade to the structure, with the result of a fatal collapse during construction. Twice extended by George Boswell, 1935 and 1936, the 1936 (southern) wing is an unusual blend of 1930s glass curtain wall, curved corners, and polychromatic tiled fascia. Entire complex converted to the Templeton Business Centre by the Charles Robertson Partnership, 1984. (Colour plate, p. 47)

C McKean

C McKean

John McKean

Above the McLennan Arch looking up Charlotte Street. *Top left* Glasgow Green in 1825. *Left* the Doulton Fountain, the Justiciary Court House, and the Briggait Steeple in the distance.

Doulton Fountain, 1888, A E Pearce

This 46 ft high terracotta fountain was the principal Doulton exhibit at the 1888 International Exhibition in Kelvingrove, re-erected on the Green after being presented to the City by Sir Henry Doulton. Observers may note that the ensemble is presided over by Queen Victoria, beneath whom four maidens empty water over the heads of soldiers and a sailor who, in turn, stand above groups representing Victoria's dominions of India, Australia, Canada and South Africa. The **Nelson Monument**, a tall obelisk that acted as the focus of the Green for many years, was designed by David Hamilton in 1806, but riven with lightning soon afterwards. The diminutive but elegant **St Andrew's Suspension Bridge** was designed by Neil Robson in 1854 for workers in Calton to reach the new industries on the south side. The **Memorial Fountain** to Hugh MacDonald, removed here from Gleniffer Braes in 1878, and erected by the Ramblers round Glasgow, may soon be adopted and revived.

Glasgow Green

'Few towns can boast such a spacious and beautiful park as the Green of Glasgow, with its wide spreading lawns, its picturesque groups of trees, its far winding walks, its numerous delicious springs and, above all, its rich command of scenery'. Thus Hugh MacDonald in 1854. The Green is central Glasgow's finest open space, its most historic and—until recently—its most neglected. Throughout history, it has been the scene of promenades, washing houses, rallies, mills, abattoirs, musters, political rallies and the celebrated Glasgow Fair. The citizens have ever had to protect it. Only 'clamorous opposition' prevented the Provost and Bailies from selling it off in 1744. In 1845, a huge petition was required to prevent a theatre opposite the Courthouse, and another two years later against a railway from crossing it. Its use as the location for much Red Clydesider oratory was ended by the authorities planting deliberately inconvenient flower beds. For the last 30 years it has been under threat of a motorway crossing.

Glasgow Fair in 1823 drawn from the roof of the Court House. Apart from the stalls on the Green itself, note St Andrew's by the Green, St Andrew's Church tower, the Tolbooth Steeple, and the old houses in Saltmarket.

13 **Justiciary Court House,** 1809-14, William Stark
In this building, Glasgow shed its antique past and the old Tolbooth in favour of purest of Grecian Doric. Won in competition it is austere to the point of Calvinism compared to the frilly, be-roundeled, fanlit and swagged collection of new public buildings in the New Town. The great stone portico, set upon a flight of steps, is strictly in accordance with the proportions of the Theseion in Athens. The Courts were entered through the portico: prisoners entered the prison through the rear. The Court House was extended by Clarke & Bell and virtually rebuilt by J H Craigie in 1913, whose handsome neo-Greek interior, with its top-lit atrium and flanking bow-ended Courts, probably re-uses some Stark material. Its original setting, on a plinth raised above the sloping river banks, gave dignity to its proportions. James Cleland became nicknamed the 'Court's gravedigger' for pushing through the new Hutchesons' Bridge, which required a new road on raised levels, destroying the building's delicate poise.

The Justiciary Court House. Note its original height at the head of two flights of steps as compared to their sunken appearance today.

DAVID DALE'S HOUSE. → CHARLOTTE ST GLASGOW DESIGNED BY ROBERT ADAM.

SCALE OF FEET.

RCAHMS

C McKean

Above elevation of Charlotte Street drawn by Douglas Smith in 1909. *Left* Charlotte Street in 1845 drawn by David Small.

Charlotte Street, 1779

A street of elegant, mercantile mansions, each with its own coach house, closed from Glasgow Green by private gates. Built on the land (and with the materials) of the abortive St James Square, each house was a variation upon the Tobacco Lord villa : a slightly raised, two-storeyed villa, its tall, steep roof behind a pediment enhanced by swagged urns, concealing a third. Principal rooms were upon the first floor. Dale's house, adjacent to the Green, was possibly designed by Robert Adam.

14 52 Charlotte Street, 1783

The most complete of the three original buildings that survive in Charlotte Street, although shorn of its coach house, and the urns which graced its pediment and corners (although the plinths remain). Its quality is clear, and the doorcase excellent. Under restoration by the National Trust for Scotland. Other houses of like vintage are **Nos 57-9** and **Nos 77-81**.

Our Lady and St Francis School,

1964, Gillespie Kidd & Coia

A fine exemplar of the more Expressionist 1960s architecture, its banded brick and concrete displaying Corbusian influence. Although typically spartan, it is far from being faceless . The elements of the building have been arranged so as to create variety, proportion and incident, and its apparent scale has been reduced cleverly by its horizontality. Well worth a detour.

David Dale, 1739-1806

Couthy, astute, tubby and generous; businessman, banker, developer, mill owner, and lay preacher, David Dale built himself the largest house in Charlotte Street in 1783, a street which he, with candlemaker Archibald Paterson, had caused to be built on the site of abandoned St James Square. Originally a journeyman from Stewarton, Ayrshire, Dale became a dealer in, and then considerable importer of linen yarn. In 1783, he brought Richard Arkwright to Scotland, with whom he founded New Lanark (his eldest daughter later married Robert Owen). His business interests included thread works, dye works, coal mining, the Royal Bank of Scotland, and mills in Perthshire and Lanarkshire. He was one of the founders of the Glasgow Chamber of Commerce. His generosity and contributions to poor relief and flood relief were legendary. For all his success, he remained a couthy Scot—someone, one could hazard, that Sir Walter Scott had in mind when creating Bailie Nicol Jarvie. His girth caused great mirth. When explaining to a friend that he had fallen '*all his length*' on ice, the friend replied: '*Be thankful, Sir, it was not your breadth!*' He is buried in the Ramshorn kirkyard.

35

ST ANDREW'S SQUARE

St Andrew's-by-the-Green.

Miller Partnership

¹⁵**St Andrew's-by-the-Green**, 1750-1,
William Paull and Andrew Hunter
An Episcopalian kirk in staunch Presbyterian
Glasgow was bad enough. This one compounded the
sin with lofts, fine panelling, seats laid with cushions
'stuffed and covered with green cloth' and—worst of
all—an organ at the west end. Music being despised
by the hardliners, this simple, pedimented and
quoined baroque box was given the opprobrious
epithet the *Whistlin' Kirkie*. Hunter, the master
mason, was excommunicated for his involvement
with this church. Converted to offices by the Miller
Partnership after years of being threatened with
removal. The adjacent red sandstone warehouse at
33-39 Greendyke Street was a rather extravagant
leather warehouse by John Keppie, 1893.

St Andrew's Church: east gable.

C. McKean

¹⁶**St Andrew's Church**, 1739-59,
Allan Dreghorn and Mungo Nasmith
Dreghorn, the city businessman, coach builder and
amateur architect, Nasmith the mason, and Thomas
Clayton the plasterer created the finest church of its
generation in Scotland (whose gigantic portico caused
such alarm that Nasmith spent the first night after
the removal of the centering sleeping beneath it to
demonstrate his faith in its stability). This towered
baroque, orange stone temple, with rusticated quoins
and magnificent cartouche on its west gable, follows
one of James Gibbs' variants on St Martin-in-the-
Fields, London. Its west end is almost entirely
portico. The interior is almost grander than its
London prototype: a huge order of Corinthian
columns supports a gallery, with bold cornices at the
springing of the vaults. The pulpit is no doubt from
Dreghorn's own workshops, whereas the remaining
furnishings are the consequence of refurbishing by
John Carrick and P Macgregor Chalmers.
(Colour plate, p. 46)

St Andrew's Church and Square.

Anne Dick

St Andrew's Square, 1786-7, William Hamilton
Authorised in 1757, the Square failed to attract a
market for another 30 years, and the church
remained in open countryside on the banks of the
Molendinar. In 1786, Hamilton, a former assistant of
Robert Adam, began his 'set of elegant modern
buildings, scarcely to be equalled anywhere in the
City.' The houses were plain, distinguished only by
fanlights, pediments and proportion. They have now
been demolished pending development. **Nos 46-8** on
the south is a leather warehouse of 1876.

Saltmarket

Originally *Waulcergait*, the Saltmarket linked
Glasgow Cross to the head of the Briggait, where the
principal route cranked west down to Glasgow
Bridge. The entry to the Green was protected by a
gateway: the *Barras Yett*. Clearly the fashionable
place to live in the early 18th century, here Sir
Walter Scott located the home of Bailie Nicol Jarvie
with 'a the comforts o' the Sautmarket' in *Rob Roy*:
and here Smollett settled Roderick Random. The
arrival of bleachfields, slaughterhouses, the Justiciary
Court and the construction of Hutchesons' Bridge in
1829 brought an end to its riverside seclusion.

Gibson's Land

After the 1677 fire, the plot on the
corner of what became later
Princes Street was rebuilt by its
merchant owner Walter Gibson. It
was described thus in 1736 by the
Glasgow historian John McUre: 'It
stands upon eighteen stately pillars
or arches, and adorn'd with the
several orders of architecture,
conform to the direction of that
great architect Sir William Bruce.
The entry consists of four several
arches toward the court thereof;
this magnificent structure is
admir'd by all forreigners and
strangers.' Gibson's Land, the
setting for Tobias Smollett's
Roderick Random, collapsed in
1823.

Saltmarket.

RCAHMS

Most of the street, now beautifully spruced up, consists of fawn sandstone City Improvement Trust tenements designed by John Carrick in 1871 (**Nos 109-27**) and by J J Burnet in 1899 (**Nos 15-27**), with a suitably crowstepped new infill on the west side. The **Ship Bank Building**, 1904, by R W Horn, aspires to a curved, carved domed tower at each end, enhanced by *aedicules* (a decoration of columns and pediment around a window to look like a miniature temple).

Nos 128-136 Bridgegate were designed in baroque red sandstone by M S Macdonald as part of a 1905 road improvement; and there is some new 'brickitecture' just beyond the railway arch (whose introduction caused the downfall of this noble thoroughfare).

Clyde Street showing Briggait on right.

C. McKean

17 **Briggait, 64-67 Clyde Street**, 1873, Clarke & Bell
Built originally as the Fish Market, eventually enveloping the steeple of the old Merchants' Hall: both elevations French in character, the screen wall to Clyde Street with twin arches set in coupled columns and surmounted by sea horses. The spacious hall has the delight of cast-iron galleries and a glazed roof. Imaginatively restored and converted by ASSIST Architects, 1985-6. (Colour plate, p. 47)

Merchants' Steeple, Bridgegate (Briggait), 1665
Although the road to the bridge is first recorded in the 12th century, it was not until the 17th that it began to attract the grander buildings. Of these, the noblest was the *Merchants' House* built on this site in 1659, of which only the *Steeple* survives. A now missing City Record stated that the designer was Sir William Bruce, although the date seems early. Glasgow was (and is) a city of towers, but this one was much more sophisticated than the others of that time, and is uncannily like (at its lower stages) some of Wren's City church towers which were to follow.

C. McKean

Merchants' House, 1659
Characteristic of the 17th-century public buildings, the House had two storeys—ground-floor shops and the principal room on the first floor, with a row of finely carved dormer windows. *The guildhall, which comprehends the length and breadth of the house, is beautified with the gilded broads, names, designations, and sums mortified for the use of poor old members of merchant rank.* In 1817 the Merchants quit the growing squalor of the district and sold their hall for the construction of a new warren, Guildry Court. They then had to endure almost 60 years of walkabout, in the new Town Hall, Virginia Street, and the City and County Buildings, before settling in George Square in 1877. The houses of rich Glasgow merchants clustered hereabouts were similar. The 1660 mansion of Campbell of Blythswood, which was located in the Briggait, was similar to the Merchants' House, Netherlandish in inspiration: long, two-storeyed, whose principal floor presented a serrated skyline of pedimented dormer windows, like jagged teeth.

Albert Bridge, 1870-1, Bell & Miller
One of the most ambitious cast-iron bridges ever built, replacing Robert Stevenson's insufficiently wide though very elegant five-arch Hutcheson Bridge of 1829-33. It has three, eight-ribbed spans with massively traceried spandrels containing the Glasgow coat-of-arms.

The Merchants' House in the early 19th century. Only the steeple survives. *Below* Glasgow's coat-of-arms on the Albert Bridge.

Victoria Bridge, 1851-4, James Walker
The finest of Glasgow's bridges, its five arches superbly executed in Kingston granite at a cost of £40,000. It replaced the medieval Glasgow bridge, built originally by Bishop Rae, c. 1345 (with the financial assistance of Lady Lochow), only 12 ft wide, where *two wheelbarrows tremble when they meet*; widened in 1776, shortened at the north end from eight arches to six and, finally, elegantly widened with iron arches over the cutwaters by Telford in 1819-21.

Anne Dick

S V Carrick, 1864
791 ton, teak-clad, iron-framed retired tea clipper, with the record of the fastest, crossing from Adelaide: achieved in 65 days. Now RNVR HQ.

C McKean

Glasgow as it was in the late 18th century. Note particularly Bob Dragon's house second left from the Bridge, and the Town's Hospital to the left of that. St Enoch's Church tower is in the distance. *Right* St Andrew's Cathedral and the new Diocesan Offices.

Old Glasgow Green

Old Glasgow, or the *Laigh* Green ran from the Molendinar to Jamaica Street, and was granted to the City from the Bishop's forest by James II in April 1450 with the rights, for those who could understand them, of *Pit and gallows, Sok, Sak, Thol, Them, Infangandthief, Outfangandthief, Hamisukken, with tenants and tenandries.* The oldest public park in Scotland, it was probably under water at each Spring Tide. In its midst, the Town located its charitable **Town's Hospital** in 1733, a large, plain, pedimented building whose purpose was a type of poor-house: '*That the poor might be better provided for than formerly, with wholesome food, good clothes, clean lodgings, and all other necessary accommodations of life at less expense than they used to stand the...for their maintenance.*'

Clyde Street

Built upon the site of Glasgow's Old Green it contained two of the finest of the pedimented, Palladian villas, then characteristic of Glasgow. The western was designed in 1752 by Allan Dreghorn for himself, with superb interior plasterwork presumably by Thomas Clayton. Now known as **Carrick Quay**, the site is planned for an adventurous block of flats in maritime style by Davis Duncan. The section of Clyde Street extending to Jamaica Street, was laid out in 1773, and contains some altered three-storey survivors, c.1810 at **228-238**. In the early 1970s, the Planning Department, with Crouch & Hogg, created the present terraced gardens and formal walkway on the site of the former transit sheds of *Custom House Quay*.

Anne Dick

18 **St Andrew's Cathedral**, 1816, James Gillespie Graham
Its Late Gothic delicacy now revealed by cleaning, this ambitious £16,000 building signalled the entry to

public life of Glasgow's rapidly growing Roman Catholic community. It was the first serious piece of Gothic revivalism in Glasgow: '*college chapel*' in form, with a neo-Perpendicular profile and curvilinear tracery. Gable to the street with traceried octagonal buttresses, and a niche at the apex containing a statue of St Andrew. Handsome plaster-vaulted interior.

54 Clyde Street, 1987, Nicholson & Jacobson
Crystalline L-plan block with blue glazed façade and masonry plinth, re-fashioned from a 1914 cork warehouse by H E Clifford.

19 **Custom House, 298 Clyde Street** , 1840, John Taylor
Greek Doric, and surprisingly modest compared with the structures reared by H M Customs at Liverpool, Greenock, Leith and Dundee. Nine bays wide, columned recessed upper storey with a superbly sculptured coat-of-arms. The set-back, Venetian-windowed bays are 20th-century additions over original yard arches. The eastern one links to a handsomely proportioned five-bay neo-classical block of similar date at **No 286**.

Bob Dragon
Robert Dreghorn of Ruchill, son of Allan (coachmaker and creator of St Andrew's Church) inherited considerable wealth and his father's Palladian mansion in West Clyde Street, at which he was thought to maintain a '*rather hospitable table surrounded often by a circle of fashionable friends*'. His nickname originated from a sadly pockmarked, wall-eyed and otherwise bent visage which is said to have inhibited his pursuit of the fair sex. He gradually attracted a reputation of peevishness and monstrosity, probably more related to his looks than his actions. He died in 1806, and his magnificent house, nicknamed Bob Dragon's house, was thenceforth reputed to be haunted.

Above Custom House. *Left* Clyde Street in the 1850s. The John Knox Church by David Hamilton on the right (demolished). *Below* Carrick Quay.

ELEVATIONS.

Top Peter Nicholson's elevation for Carlton Place. *Middle* the stairwell in John Laurie's house. *Above* Carlton Place Suspension Bridge.

[20] **Laurieston House**, 1802, Peter Nicholson
The centre of this fine terrace is the pedimented pair which comprised the mansions of John and David Laurie: a strangely two-dimensional façade which looked better when the whole terrace was in fine stonework (as compared to its currently prettily coloured paint). The scale is broad, but the details very shallow (the very early Greek pilasters supporting the pediment are almost invisible)—the only relief being a shallow, bowed and balustraded Doric porch. Restoration of the stonework and originally proportioned window glazing bars now under way by Philip Cocker & Partners. Inside, the rich details echo those of Robert Adam and Sir John Soane. The Corinthian-columned staircases with domed rotundas are particularly fine.

Sheriff Court, 1985, Keppie Henderson & Partners
A large, grey, shiny slab, its plain rectangular columns doing little to modulate its scale; yet a fine and complex double-height space within like the foyer of a national theatre, with excellent use of colour and sculpture. It is as though two different design teams had worked on the project. The green-glazed dome of the nearby **Mosque**, completed in 1985 by Coleman Ballantine, has become one of the city's landmarks.

Carlton Place Suspension Bridge, 1851-3, Alexander Kirkland
A singularly ambitious footbridge, built to connect the city centre with Portland Street. The Greek Ionic pylons were by Alexander Kirkland, the 414-ft span by George Martin. *Owing to insufficiency of estimates, and defects arising from bad materials and workmanship the first towers had to be taken down and rebuilt and for a long time grave doubts were entertained as to its stability.* These doubts were dispelled in 1871 by radical strengthening at the hands of Bell & Miller.

Jamaica Bridge, 1833 (reconstructed), Thomas Telford
Granite, with a much lower rise than Old Glasgow Bridge, it was rebuilt in widened form to designs by

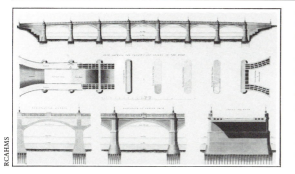

RCAHMS

Cunningham, Blyth & Westland between 1894 and 1899. It is still substantially Telford's as his granite facings and balustrades (the balusters of which were then polished) were re-used. Cunningham Blyth & Westland's hand is evident mainly at the piers which are pierced by arches and have a different capping at the parapet. Of the original, three-span wrought-iron lattice girder **Central Station viaduct** by Blyth & Cunningham, 1876-8, only the Dalbeattie granite piers remain.

Carlton Place
In 1794 John and David Laurie bought land belonging to Hutchesons' Hospital (hence Hutchesontown), the Trades Hospital (hence Tradeston) and the Council itself. They laid out large blocks of classical tenements and houses facing wide streets named after aristrocracy or Royalty—such as Cumberland, Portland, Carlton, Cavendish, Bedford, Norfolk and Oxford. It was probably the most ambitious—and least successful—new town planning to occur in Glasgow. The hinterland was never fully developed, and the scheme became hemmed in by ironworks and then cut by railways. The finest survivor—and the best of its type in Glasgow—is Carlton Place, designed 1802-4 by Peter Nicholson. With Portland Street, it was Glasgow's Harley Street for most of the 19th century.

Top left Telford's design for Jamaica Bridge from 1833. *Left* looking east past Jamaica Bridge to the Broomielaw in the 1850s.

Mitchell Library

BROOMIELAW
Nos 54-72 (now distillers but originally the shipowners J & P Hutchison's), 1878, was the grandest of the shipping offices: tall with triple arched and pedimented dormers. The monumental, Corinthian-pilastered façade of **Nos 2-12** by Alexander Skirving, 1883, flanks the approach to the city at Jamaica Bridge.

Jamaica Bridge or more correctly Glasgow Bridge, was planned by the magistrates as part of a scheme to extend the town beyond the West Port, in co-operation with the Merchants' House. The foundation stone of the original bridge (designed by Robert and William Mylne, built by John Adam of Glasgow and completed in 1772 at a cost of almost £9000) was laid with great ceremony by Provost George Murdoch in 1767, the procession leaving not from the Town Hall but from the Saracen's Head in Gallowgate.

C McKean

Above and below Clyde Port Authority.
Right Second Trust Hall, Clyde Port Authority.

George V Bridge, 1924-8, Thomas Somers
Elegant reinforced concrete bridge with only three spans (146 ft and 110 ft) of very low-rise continuous beams, resting on cast-steel roller bearings independent of the substructure. Faced with Dalbeattie granite and a balustraded parapet on the model of Jamaica and Glasgow bridges. Its cost was five times that of the Albert Bridge half a century earlier, illustrating that inflation is nothing new.

Oswald Street, from 1800
Mostly original four-storey tenements of 1810-25 vintage survive on the west side. Note **Richey's Leisure, No 11**, 1844, with its tall pilastered and pedimented façade. The steel offices at **No 35** were designed by J J Craig in 1909 for Stewart & Menzies (later Stewart & Lloyd's Clyde Tube Works).

Robertson Street
A large, rubble c.1800 warehouse lies within the court at **No 51** with a pedimented, projecting front, the small, square blank windows added later for a stair. The two-storey Italian Romanesque block, **Nos 45-49**, built in 1869 for the engineer James Gilchrist, is distinctive for its galleried engineering shop. It was a work of art, its travelling crane running on the handrail of its highly ornamental balustrading.

Anne Dick

21 **Clyde Port Authority**, 16 Robertson Street, from 1882, J J Burnet
The Clyde Navigation Trust rivalled the Town Council in power and influence, and its headquarters were of comparable grandeur. What we see now is only two of the four stages originally intended, which would have given the building a frontage almost as large as that of the City Chambers. The five-bay pedimented unit, surmounted by a colossal statue of Neptune by John Mossman, was intended as the

Top panorama of Glasgow by John Knox (courtesy Glasgow Museums and Art Galleries). *Right* the interior of St Andrew's Church. *Bottom* Glasgow Bridges and the Merchants' Tower by J Brooks, 1806 (Glasgow Museums and Art Galleries).

OPPOSITE Templeton's Carpet Factory — detail from the main façade. *Top right* Glasgow from Glasgow Green, a painter from the Scottish School (c. 1820). *Middle right* James Watt's house, Broomielaw, painted by William Simpson. *Bottom right* the Briggait.

Glasgow Museums and Art Galleries

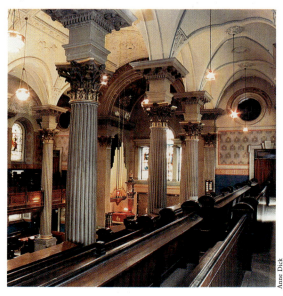

Anne Dick

Glasgow Museums and Art Galleries

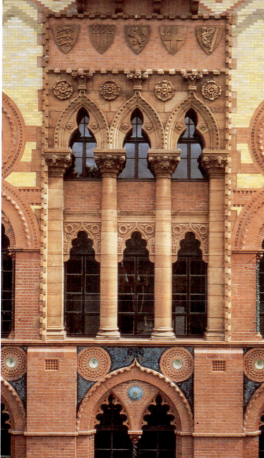

Hunterian Art Gallery

Glasgow City Libraries

Top Clyde Street at night. *Above* Glasgow Bridge painted by Sam Bough. The steeple of St Enoch's Church rises above the Customs House to the right.

48

centre of a huge composition, extending up Robertson Street, of which Burnet published a dreamy watercolour (showing a Venetian campanile turning the corner into Broomielaw), in 1888. In 1906 he replaced the campanile by a subtly Frenchified dome, with imposing sculpture groups of Europa and Amphitrite by Albert Hodge. The interiors are among the most sophisticated in Glasgow. Beyond the domed entrance loggia, the floor level continues to rise processionally, into a square, clerestoried green and gold business hall with banded Doric columns. The huge grand stair, lit at the foot by a stupendous lamp standard with Roman prow cantilever brackets, leads to principal apartments on the second floor; approached along a sumptuous corridor of domelets supported on black pilasters with gold-leaf Corinthian capitals. The Old Trust Hall is a superb example of French taste of the 1870s and 1880s. The Second Trust Hall, a domed rotunda, has a mahogany wainscot wall divided into eight bays by white marble Ionic columns. (Colour plate, p. 45)

71-75 Robertson Street, 1899, John A Campbell
Five-storey red stone office building, with a Doric eaves gallery, and a circular corner tower corbelled out to a sculptural octagon, with a broad-eaved ogee roof. Banded brickwork elevations to Robertson Lane, and the white glazed brick rear, can teach Post-Modernists much.

64 Robertson Street, 1902-5, Andrew Balfour
Doric giant-arched entrance and a central oriel set between recessed Corinthian columns; built for Wm McLeod & Co, metal merchants and founders' factors.

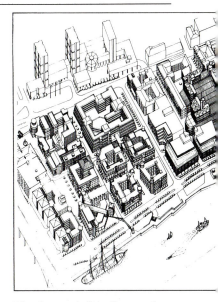

The *Campus de Bromilaw* was first mentioned about 1325. The removal of a ford downstream c.1556 enabled a pier and a small port to be built, and by 1589 it had become so busy that magistrates held coble courts there. In 1724, a timber-faced quay was built, *so large that a regiment of horses may be exercised thereon*, and by 1800, streets were being laid out running northward to Argyle Street. The Broomielaw developed as a handsome waterfront parade of tall shipping-related buildings punctuated by the mighty dome of the Clyde Navigation Trust and the lighthouse-like corner tower of the Italianate Sailors' Home. As ships increased in size, cargo business had to move down river replaced by a corresponding increase in passenger business, the quayside becoming crowded with very fast paddle-steamers jostling for a berth. Precious little of that former maritime bustle remains now beyond the Clyde Port Authority and, when berthed at the Quay, *PS Waverley*. The *doon the watter* commuters now go by car.

The Broomielaw, drawn by Robert Eadie in 1926. *Above* scheme for the new Broomielaw by BDP and the Holmes Partnership.

Until 1969 Cheapside Street was the site of Henry Houldsworth's remarkable Anderston Cotton Works, built 1804-6. The first fireproof, iron-framed structure in Scotland, three-aisled with brick jack arches, it was clearly the work of an original mind. Its severe, temple-like brick façade bore Doric pilasters five storeys high, carrying an impressive entablature. Steam-heat was provided through hollow cores in its columns.

York Street, laid out 1802
Villas and a riding school soon gave way to large warehouses for grain, tea and whisky. The most impressive is the 17-bay **Queen's Tea Store (No 23)**, by John Stephen in 1843 for William Connal, which is distinguished by a central archway of bizarre profile and three tall arched windows. **Nos 13 & 15 York Street**, 1897, by W F MacGibbon (now Henry Afrika's) is a pretty, Flemish-gabled conception. The seven-storey baroque façade with Corinthian columns of **74 York Street**, 1898-1901, by Neil C Duff, exemplifies the grandeur to which a fish gut company could then aspire.

22 **James Watt Street**, from 1849, John Stephen
The name commemorates James Watt's pedimented villa which previously occupied the site (Colour page 11). The central part is entirely composed of grandly architectural warehouses, the finest being **Nos 44-54**, 1861, enormous 13-bay palace front, with three-bay pilastered and pedimented end pavilions. Above a rusticated ground floor, the middle two storeys read as one, their windows joined in huge recessed openings. Continuous pilastered frieze pierced by

The warehouses in James Watt Street; Nos 44-54 on right, Nos 68-72 beyond.

small square attic windows. The rustication and frieze were carefully lined up with that of **68-72** built in 1847-8 for William Connal, presumably also by John Stephen. **Nos 65-73**, c. 1848, old-fashioned Greek Revival with giant pilasters running up through four of the five storeys at the pedimented centrepiece and at the end bays.

Tobacco Warehouse, 41-45 James Watt Street, 1854, John Baird
Two-storey, with a raised three-storey pedimented centre with sculpture by John Mossman, heightened to six storeys in 1910-11 by Baird & Thomson. Externally stone; reinforced concrete within. Now a hire store.

Marine Police Office, MacAlpine Street, 1882, John Carrick
Old-fashioned 1850s Italian: arched and channelled ground floor, and recessed Doric doorpiece.

Washington Street
A street of grain mills and stores, cooperages, bonded stores, a sugar refinery and, many years ago, the headquarters of Walter Macfarlane's Saracen Ironworks which occupied a fine Venetian building by Boucher & Cousland. The stone-built part of **No 27** is an early cotton store converted in 1865 to the Anderston Grain Mills when the tall arcaded block of red and yellow brick was added.

H E Clifford's **Washington Street School**, 1890, is now an arts complex. Note the wheatsheaf at the top of **Crown Flour Mills**, 1866, next to a still impressive remnant of the Doric-pilastered Washington Grain Mills of 1874. **Buchanan's Bond**, Washington Street, 1897, by Alexander Gardner is a colossal, red sandstone, arcaded pile, extended 1906 by H E Clifford. Currently under restoration.

Howard Street, from 1789
Original plain early 19th-century four-storey tenements survive at **Nos 40-58**. McCorquodale's Printing Works, **No 70**, built in instalments from 1868 onwards, has a bowed corner to Maxwell Street, and elevations modelled by plain pilastrades. The tall, triple-arched, red sandstone 1903 warehouse was designed for leather by Andrew Balfour; and the boldly designed warehouse at **118-120**, 1903-4, by John Gibb Morton (an architect of great promise who emigrated to Canada shortly thereafter), draws on motifs from Mackintosh, Salmon, Burnet and Campbell with considerable success.

Anne Dick

Tobacco warehouse, 41-45 James Watt Street.

The establishment of a theatre in Glasgow had been fraught with difficulty. One was built against the Archbishop's Castle in 1750 but, preaching in the adjoining High Church Yard in 1754, the Rev George Whitfield denounced it as a *Devil's House*; whereupon his congregation tore it down. In 1762 the comedians Love, Jackson and Beate promoted another theatre; fired by its audience on its opening night. Repaired and refitted, it survived until 1782 when it was allowed to burn out completely, the Magistrates devoutly declining to frustrate the will of God by ordering the firemen to play their hoses only on the adjoining houses. In 1784-5, Jackson built the first Dunlop Street Theatre, in which Mrs Siddons and Mrs Jordan appeared. When the Queen Street Theatre was burned in 1829, that in Dunlop Street was first improved to take the place of both; and then completely rebuilt in 1839-40 on a scale comparable with that in Queen Street, to designs by William Spence. Its façade was grandly Doric with much statuary, Shakespeare being flanked by Garrick and the proprietor, the actor-manager John Henry Alexander. It was demolished in 1866 for St Enoch Station, the name being transferred to the new theatre at the top of Hope Street (see p. 110).

Above St Enoch's Travel Centre, drawn by Arthur McLeod.

St Enoch was—somewhat surprisingly—female, the name being corrupted by the glottal stop from 'St Thenaw'. The unmarried daughter of King Loth of Traprain, in the Lothians, she was cast adrift pregnant, to make landfall at Culross. Her son St Mungo, or Kentigern, the patron saint of Glasgow, thus turns out to be the illegitimate son of a single parent.

1906 Royal (formerly National) Bank.

St Enoch Square, from 1782
Like St Andrew's Square, laid out around a pre-existing church of the same name: a pleasant, steepled, 1770 box kirk by James Jaffray, replaced in 1827-8 by a noble classical church by David Hamilton (although keeping Jaffray's steeple). It closed the vista down Buchanan Street until its demolition in 1925.

23 **Travel Centre**, 1896, James Miller
A pretty, diminutive Jacobean pavilion, like a toy version of Azay-le-Rideau in red sandstone—the architectural mascot of the Underground system—its scale was determined by the need not to compete with the church behind.

46-64 St Enoch Square, 1895, Alexander Petrie
One of the earliest of Glasgow's really large elevator buildings: six-storey, *fin-de-siècle* red sandstone office block with shallow oriels.

Royal Bank of Scotland, 22-24, 1906,
A N Paterson
Five storeys capped by a pedimented attic, most of the Beaux-Arts architectural excitement at the top. Figures of Prudence, Adventure, Commerce and Security over the side entrances are by Phyllis Archibald.

26-30 St Enoch's Square, c.1880
Originally a cast-iron façade capped by corbelled Venetian Romanesque dormer windows, the iron was replaced by its present mullioned grid in 1932. The **Royal Bank of Scotland (26-36)**, c.1876, similarly rises into a machicolated cornice and a French pavilion roof. The sophisticated Italianate four lower storeys of **Nos 28-48**, by Robert Thomson, c.1870, have sculptured pediments. The top floor is arcaded under a deep bracketed cornice.

William Teacher's, 14 St Enoch's Square, 1875, James Boucher
Light, cosmopolitan, four storeys of arched Italianate, round-headed windows, articulated into 2-3-2 bays. Each floor distinctive. Channelled stonework, ironwork balcony, and sculptured spandrels.

St Enoch station was the Glasgow & South Western's northern counterpart to St Pancras. Gothic hotel and offices by Thomas Willson, an obscure Catholic church architect from Hampstead, rivalled St Pancras only in sheer extent; but Sir John Fowler and J F Blair's great arched roof (204 ft wide

C McKean

Anne Dick

RCAHMS

Stuart Baxter

Stuart Baxter

compared to St Pancras's 243 ft) was very sophisticated. Now covered by an even larger glass roof, the site houses the **St Enoch's Centre**, a massive U-plan shopping centre and ice-rink, by Reiach & Hall with GMW Architects, wrapped around a seven-storey car park. Note shiny, tube-like decoration of the façade of the car park to Osborne Street.

St Enoch's Square: *Top left* as original, Surgeons' Hall (1791) by James Craig on left. *Above* two views of the St Enoch's Shopping development. *Centre left* 14 St Enoch's Square. *Bottom left* the original railway station arches.

RCAHMS

Martin & Frost, formerly Gardner's Warehouse, in which the lessons of the Crystal Palace in London were adapted for a normal commercial building. Nos 30-34 on right.

Jamaica Street, opened 1763
Planned in 1751 as the approach to the new bridge, Jamaica Street originally comprised mainly four-storey tenements, and one great Palladian villa, that of George Buchanan of Hillington, on the east side just south of Adam Court (demolished 1849). Redevelopment of the remainder of the street followed very quickly, and within a few years it had become the scene of some of the most exciting experiments in iron construction in the United Kingdom.

2-10 Jamaica Street
Four-storey, early 19th century tenement on the corner of Argyle Street, notable (until 1988 refurbishment) mainly for the all-glass fifth floor with just the slimmest of timber and T-pattern window divides, in the manner of Alexander Thomson. The **Classic Grand, 18-22**, originally an 1860 three-storey warehouse of identical superimposed pilasters, crowned by an arcaded eaves

gallery, was converted to a cinema in 1915 by William B Whitie.

30-34 Jamaica Street, 1864, John Honeyman. Proudly Venetian. Two storeys of superimposed Ionic and Corinthian columns forming round arched, recessed windows, sitting on a plinth of heavily rusticated pilasters, presumably like the surviving entrance. It has a particular place in Glasgow's mercantile history, being built as the headquarters of G & J Burns, joint founder of the Cunard Line.

24 **Martin & Frost, 36 Jamaica Street**, 1855-6, John Baird I
Gardner's Warehouse is one of the great landmarks of Western architectural history, being the first in which the lessons of the Crystal Palace's prefabricated structure were applied successfully to everyday building. The structural frame was designed by R McConnell who held the patent for its wrought and cast iron beams. The detailing of the delicate, cast-iron, arcaded and almost transparent façades, with their beautifully integrated timber lettering added later, was by Baird.

MacSorley's Bar, 1898-99, Clarke & Bell
Five storeys of American brownstone realised in red sandstone, the Art Nouveau glazing unfortunately all that survives of the ground floor bar. Its American character may have been directly due to Philip MacSorley, who had a famous New York Bar and imported *an expert barman from New York* to operate his Glasgow one.

60-66 Jamaica Street, 1856-7, Hugh Barclay
Second of Jamaica Street's great iron monuments: eight slim bays of iron-framed glazing, recessed within three giant semi-elliptical arches, crowned by a great cornice cantilevered out on ornate cast-iron console brackets. The **Colosseum**, a toughly detailed 1860s building, has all the punch of which that decade was capable. The iron construction of **No 72**, 1854, by William Spence, is probably the earliest in Glasgow by about a year; nine bays of four-colonnaded storeys of slim iron columns, and a balustraded parapet. Masonry pilasters only at the ends.

Until the great fire of 1988, the east side of Jamaica Street comprised several monuments of Victorian commerce. The only survivor is **Nos 25-27**, an 1875 version of the common post-Thomson package of rows of pilasters above each other, an arcaded eaves gallery, and pedimented dormer windows.

RIAS Library

60-66 Jamaica Street: another of the iron pioneers.

Tolbooth Steeple.

[25]GLASGOW CROSS

Tolbooth Steeple, 1626, John Boyd
A crown-helmeted, stone traffic policeman,
surrounded by roads (which threatened to run over
it), the steeple is the sole relict of Glasgow's new
Tolbooth which symbolised the advancing mercantile
power of the city. The steeple has a splendid
verticality, only string courses, buckle quoins,
mouldings around the door, and small windows for
decoration.

Glasgow Cross, 1920-32, A Graham Henderson
West quadrant of a frigidly classical competition-
winning scheme to enclose the Cross with a vast
semicircle of steel-framed, stone-clad mercantile
premises. The east quadrant was not built (although
a fine, tall, corniced, post-modern rectangle of flats
and shops by McGurn Logan Duncan & Opfer is
currently being considered); leaving the **Mercat
Building**, 1922, by Graham Henderson (the concave
hollow (exedra) behind the pillars cleverly floodlit at
night) isolated and without context. The Cross
requires to be re-sealed.

Mercat Cross, 1930, Edith Burnet Hughes
Old Scots: an octagonal base with raised, balustraded
platform surmounted by finial and heraldic beast.

Trongate was the principal thoroughfare of Glasgow
Tobacco Lords, who were apt to saunter upon the
'plainstanes' in front of their Coffee Room and
Exchange, and remove others not so entitled with
their sticks. This was Glasgow's *'Rialto'*. Its
stateliness departed with the merchant emigration
westwards and, latterly, the growth of traffic.
Carriage trade moved to Buchanan Street, and thence
to Sauchiehall Street. The Trongate changed from
being the promenade of the Quality to what it is
now: the *people's street*. Arcades began to disappear in
the late 18th century, replaced by large, plain
classical New Town buildings, of which **Nos
130-136**, known as the Old Post Office Close,
c.1790, still survives. A riot of Victorian commercial
exuberance superseded them, the final phase being
the post-1872 redevelopments, by the City
Improvement Trust at the eastern end with their
sandstone tenements.

Town Hall (demolished), 1737-40, Allan Dreghorn
Unusually sophisticated sign of Glasgow's growing
wealth, with close similarities to both Somerset
House and to Covent Garden. Windows of the

West Quadrant, Glasgow Cross.

Mitchell Library

The Four Young men of talent

In 1788 Sir John Dalrymple recorded a conversation held with Provost Andrew Cochrane of Glasgow '*as to what causes he imputed the sudden rise of Glasgow. He said it was all owing to four young men of talent and spirit who started up at one time in business'.* They were John Glassford of Dougalston, William Cunninghame of Lainshaw, Alexander Spiers of Elderslie, and James Ritchie of Craigton; all involved in the Virginia Trade. Cunninghame's mansion survives encased within the Royal Exchange (see p. 88). The Tobacco Lords dressed in imitation of Venetian and Genoese merchants in scarlet cloaks, curled wigs, cocked hats and gold headed canes. No person not of their body was allowed to address them without first being invited to do so.

Left the Trongate drawn by Robert Paul in the 1760s. *Top* the Town Hall. *Bottom* Section through the Town Hall and the Tontine Coffee House behind, drawn by Alexander Hay.

The front of the Tontine *and the coffee room under the piazzas were the great daily rendezvous of the leading notables of the community; and at the upper end of that so celebrated newsroom, to be considered a sight for all strangers, were always congregated from one to three o'clock, those who either were the acknowledged—or else imagined themselves to be—dons of the city. These daily meetings were not, as might be supposed, for exchange of business matters, but merely for gossiping or, what was equally important, for arranging where they should dine, or at what hour the particular club of which they were members should assemble. The pacers of the newsroom boards were a jolly-looking, well-dressed, red-faced, gentlemen-like set of fellows, with a roar and a laugh always at command, and a sort of independent swagger, bespeaking full purses and no backwardness in opening them. Hospitality was their ruling characteristic* ' (of 1793: Dr John Strang).

Mitchell Library

Right the Trongate drawn by Samuel Brown in 1774. The gigantic portico on the left fronted the Guard House — hence the soldiers parading in front. The arcaded fronts of the earlier houses can be seen in the distance.

principal chamber, at first floor sitting above a rusticated loggia, were identified by triangular and segmental pediments. Giant Ionic pilasters supported a balustraded and urned parapet. In 1758-60, a further five bays were added to the west. The keystones of the arcades were carved with human heads and grotesques, and were known as the 'Tontine Heads'. The **Tontine Hotel and Coffee Room** by William Hamilton, 1781, often confused with the Town Hall, were built by public subscription to the rear; and the arcades which supported the Town Hall were opened up and used as a loggia or piazza for the new 74 ft long coffee room *'universally allowed to be the most elegant of its kind in Britain if not in Europe'*.

Tontine site, Trongate, 1905, Robert Sandilands Elephantine red sandstone warehouses with shallow, repetitive details—such as triplets of windows framed by giant Ionic pilasters, marginally enlivened by a magnificent baroque dome.

Nos 3-39 Trongate, 1891, M S MacDonald Based on an 1877 improvement planned by John Carrick, the design is outmoded Renaissance, with circled corners and truncated cone roofs.

Below J T Rochead's design for business chambers in the Trongate.

26 **Nos 42-70 Trongate**, 1854, J T Rochead The designer of the Wallace Monument employing furious turreted Baronial for the ill-fated City of Glasgow Bank. The architecture was intended to complement ancient buildings then surviving in the locality. West of it, a few later Georgian buildings survive, most notably Old Post Office Close, and two interesting mid-century attempts at glazed iron façades: **Nos 140-144**, c.1875, have three bays of

C. McKean

slim cast-iron mullions between idiosyncratic
Corinthian pilasters; **Nos 170-174**, c.1860, features
four severe storeys of triplicated windows.

27 **Tron Kirk,** Steeple, 1631; Church, 1793, James Adam
The sturdy four-stage steeple, with its Gothic
windows and heavy Scots spire, was added to the
1485 Collegiate Church of St Mary (converted to a
civic kirk in 1586). The arches were pierced through
the steeple by John Carrick in 1855, when he erected
the Jacobean edifice alongside. The old kirk was
burnt by 18th-century equivalents of lager louts on
8 February 1793, and replaced with a James Adam
box, separated from and behind the tower, which
contemporaries thought '*a fine modern building
crowned by a handsome glass dome*'. Cleverly
converted into the **Tron Theatre** by McGurn Logan
Duncan. Its name derives from the Public Weighing
Machine (or Tron) which was located just outside.
Beautiful neo-baroque 1899 screen wall by J J Burnet
to the east, built as part of the underground railway
works.

Nos 79-83 Trongate, 1896, M S MacDonald
Huge Scottish baronial tenement turning the corner
into King Street. To its east, the former **Britannia
Music Hall** designed by Gildard & MacFarlane in
1857. Originally the **Panopticon**, the music hall still
survives, like the Sleeping Beauty, in the upper
floors of this splendid Italianate confection.

King Street, from 1720s
Location of the city's first markets and some fine
classical buildings, but subsequently victim of railway
slums and reconstruction. The flamboyance of J T

James Adam's design for the Tron Kirk.

Soane Museum

James Adam's original design for
the Tron Kirk comprised a
triumphal frontage facing the
Trongate. It contained shops
within its triumphal arch centrepiece. Either money was not
forthcoming, or it was realised that
fashion was moving away from the
Tron to the New Town.

Rochead's 1849 Italianate corner with the Trongate is a false dawn to the McKissack red sandstone Improvement Trust warehouses and tenements with baroque details, which lie behind.

South of the Trongate, the old city was in trouble by the early 19th century from a mixture of conflicting uses (eg houses next to the slaughterhouse), and from overcrowding. The equivalent to the University's departure for Gilmorehill was when the merchants quit their House in the Briggait in 1817, leaving only its spire. The area's residual character is that of post-1872 slum-clearance tenements and warehouses for the City Improvement Trust, which comprise most of Chisholm, Parnie and King Streets, as well as the Briggait and Stockwellgait.

Trongate's surviving older buildings are engagingly commercial, as Glasgow wealth bought Italianate fashion in sometimes illiterate quantity. The 1885 warehouse (**Nos 137-139**) by James Sellars and the 1860 warehouse at **Nos 151-155** in its Italian palazzo, with its first-floor segmented window heads are above average.

Tobacco from Virginia

The first Glasgow-owned vessel crossed to America in 1718, and by 1721 the canny Scots merchants had developed a way of making unrivalled profits: namely carrying full cargoes in each direction. By 1735, there were 15 Glasgow-owned ships, and the city merchants chartered many others. By 1772, Glasgow imported 60% of all tobacco entering the United Kingdom, and the city exported to France, Holland and Germany. Three-quarters of the tobacco came from Virginia, some from Maryland, and a tiny amount from North Carolina. In 1772 over 45 million lb of tobacco were imported into the Clyde. Immediately before the American War of Independence brought disaster, John Glassford of Dougalston had 25 ships involved in the trade which earned him half a million pounds sterling. When the new Republic repudiated all debts, Glasgow was owed £1 million sterling and was only saved from bankruptcy by 'King Cotton'.

CANDLERIGGS

Straight, narrow and historic street, the vista closed by the Ramshorn Kirk at the top, which encapsulates much of old Glasgow. The Candlerig was opened c.1679 as the route from the Trongate north to where the candlemakers had been relocated after the 1677 fire. When the new St David's (or Ramshorn) Kirk, was opened in 1724, it was placed axially at the head. The magistrates had planned to lay out other *'new and regular streets'*, but the City's economy was so damaged by the Malt Tax Riots and the subsequent reparations made to Campbell of Shawfield whose house had been burnt, that the plans came to nothing.

1-15 and **4-69 Candleriggs**, c.1790, J & W Carswell Important survivors of early Merchant City warehouses, albeit much altered. The Carswells, who built most of it, are recorded as the first Glasgow builders to use structural cast-iron. **Nos 107-123** are marginally later. **Nos 87-99** by Thomson & Sandilands in 1912 are notable for their splendid cast-iron gates. Candleriggs became known for the quality of the warehouses—eg Rattrays—and the market which, until the early 1970s, dominated the entire Merchant City (in the same way as Covent Garden in London).

Anne Dick

Below City Hall, Albion Street frontage.
Bottom the Bazaar when still in use.

C McKean

John Gillies

Nova, 71 Candleriggs,

1931, James Taylor Thomson
The west side of the northern block of Candleriggs forms part of the Ingram Square development and the original terraces have been converted into flats by Elder & Cannon. This fine inter-war corner building has a grand corner tower and winged motif. Most of the modern architecture is reserved for the interior of the Square and the Wilson Street frontage, but the adjacent building to the tower is pedimented not dissimilar to an aggrandised Babbity Bowster's.

28 **City Hall,** from 1817, James Cleland
Pleasing Italianate hall and market, converted back to Glasgow's principal concert hall after the destruction of St Andrew's Halls (see p. 170). The bazaar was designed by Cleland, and the galleried hall over it by George Murray (who also designed the Egyptian entrance in Albion Street) in 1840. The Corinthian pilastered, round-windowed centrepiece of the Candleriggs frontage, and the staircase within are by John Carrick, 1885. The **Fruit Market** occupying the Bell St frontage is exuberantly eclectic—fluted Ionic columns, and carved roundels by J A T Houston, 1907. An even finer galleried market hall by Carrick, 1852, has a superb arched roof. Perhaps the revival of the Merchant City will bring an appropriate new use.

Shawfield Mansion,
1711, Colen Campbell
Erected by Daniel Campbell of
Shawfield at the then western
extremity of Glasgow, axially sited
to face down Stockwell Street.
Colen Campbell described it thus:
The principal apartment is in the
first storey. The staircase is so placed
in the middle as to serve four good
apartments in the second storey. The
front is dressed with Rustics of large
proportions, and a Doric cornice and
balustrade. Colen Campbell, a
lawyer whose first design this was,
went on to become the doyen of
British architecture with the
publication of his volumes
Vitruvius Britannicus and the
design of notable Palladian
buildings in England. The nearest
prototype of the Shawfield
Mansion was James Smith's lovely
Strathleven House, by Dumbarton
(which survives yet). In 1725, the
mansion was attacked and
plundered by the Glasgow mob,
since Daniel Campbell, MP for the
Glasgow Burghs, was believed to
have voted for the introduction of a
new Malt Tax. With his enormous
Government compensation of
£9,000, Campbell purchased Islay
and sold his Glasgow house to the
McDowalls of Castle Semple and
Garthland (see *The South Clyde*
Estuary in this series), who sold it
to the tobacco family Glassford.

Right Shawfield Mansion from *Vitruvius*
Britannicus. Below Glassford Court and
61-65 Glassford Street.

Stockwell Street
Principal route to the river and Glasgow's only
Bridge until 1772. The home of wealthy merchants,
No. 28, 1678, retained its protuberant dormer
windows and crowsteps until its demolition in 1978.
Nos 133-158 are marginally more vivid MacDonald
Improvement Trust tenements of 1905. Further
street widening occurred between the Wars, when
Burnet & Boston designed the red sandstone
warehouses, **Nos 5-43**, identified by the copper dome
at the corner of Trongate.

Mitchell Library

Glassford Street, from 1791
Feued through the house and gardens of the
Shawfield Mansion, then owned by the Glassford
family (hence the name of the street), it was built as
four-storey houses upon arcades. Later, it became the
favoured haunt of banks—particularly David
Hamilton's Ship Bank, and James Sellars' City of
Glasgow Bank, infamous for its crash during
construction in 1878.

29 **Royal Bank**, 1902, T P Marwick
Altogether very jolly. The stylistic origin of this
tower-house, a turret at each corner, is Marwick's
reworking of J J Burnet's unsuccessful entry for
Edinburgh's North British Hotel. A pot pourri:
baroque for its first three floors, a columned gallery
linking the turrets above, with florid Flemish gables
rising into a French room. (Colour plate, p. 103)

Warehouse, 61-65 Glassford Street, 1908,
Robertson & Dobbie
Rather splendid, tall, steel-framed warehouse tower in
the normal red sandstone, but with Art Nouveau
motifs. On the opposite corner of Wilson Street is
Thomson, Sandilands & MacLeod's tall, Ionic-

MLDO

pilastered Glen & Davidson warehouse of 1936.
Glassford Court, 37-41 Glassford Street, 1988, by
McGurn Logan Duncan and Opfer, a five-storey red
brick block of flats and shops, contains echoes of
New Town façades in a contemporary manner:
symmetry, central (post-modern) pediment, and
arcades once more at street level. The 1860
warehouse at **No 44** sports some weak pilasters and
second-floor arches. The new **Halifax Building
Society**, 1985, by Frank Burnet Bell is a
composition of polished lozenges.

30 **Trades House**, begun 1791, Robert Adam
'The increasing respectability of the Trades Rank'
required premises grander and more sophisticated
than the late medieval parsonage of Morebattle in the
upper town. Really a centre for charitable works and
administration, the House contained the statutory
70 ft pilastered hall within (many Glasgow public
buildings of this time had roughly that size of hall
for the principal room). The façade, somewhat
diminished by its neighbours, offers an Ionic
centrepiece with a dome, raised on a plinth, with
projecting flanking bays—all of which would look
better if the fanlights above the large Venetian
windows were restored. Good mouldings, carvings of
the City's arms, and griffins. Interiors remodelled by
James Sellars, 1888; John Keppie, 1916; and Walter
Underwood, 1955. The Hall was designed to face
down Garth (formerly Garthland, after the
McDowalls of Castle Semple and Garthland) Street.
The vista down Garth Street, with its plain 18th-
century, pedimented gabled buildings, still represents
the nearest to the original New Town atmosphere.

Mitchell Library

The Trades House: *Below* Adam's
original design. *Bottom* as built. *Bottom
left* the Great Hall as drawn by
Alexander Hay.

Soane Museum

John McKean

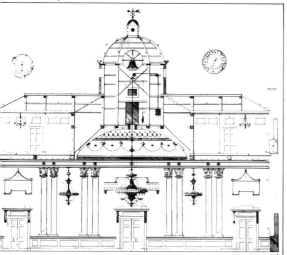

C McKean

Provost Murdoch was a member of the Hodge Podge Club, like most of those who controlled the city at the time. His colleagues serenaded him thus:

'Easy Murdoch comes sauntering, as
if in a dream
Who strives with the current but
follows the stream:
In your voyage through life, Peter,
choose your friends well
'Tis in their *power to lead you to*
heaven or hell.'

Above the Buck's Head Hotel built as Provost Murdoch's house in 1757. *Below* Alexander Thomson's replacement.

Anne Dick

Argyle Street

The removal of the West Port in 1751 is held to presage the period of civilised expansion, when wealthy Glaswegians were no longer prepared to tolerate having to entertain in their tenement bedrooms. When the Mercantile Lords took feus of the new land, they built villas in the new mode, complete with new-fangled reception rooms. The Westergait, renamed Argyle in homage to the Duke, received added impetus after 1763, when it was used as a principal thoroughfare to Jamaica Street and the new bridge. Four-storey tenements of fairly consistent design intermingled with Palladian villas and crow-stepped cottages. Only the tenement fronting the Argyle Arcade now remains in anything like its original condition.

1-11 Argyle Street, 1986-7,
Scott Brownrigg & Turner
Red sandstone Post-Modern, more sensitive to the character of Glasgow than most, although a storey too low. Note the pedimented bays, string courses and free standing columns.

31 Buck's Head Building, 63 Argyle Street,
1862, Alexander Thomson
An extraordinary construction of exposed iron stanchions and stone pilastrades, the curved angle held together by iron ring beams. Windows are glazed directly into the pilasters, giving purity of contrast between solid and void. The beams were McConnel's patent (cf 36 Jamaica Street and Nos 217-221 Argyle Street). The name recalls the Buck's Head Hotel, which occupied the impressive 1757 villa of Provost Murdoch at the site of the old West Port.

Lewis's, 1932, G de Courcey Fraser
Portland stone inter-war Manchester classic, occupying the whole block between Dunlop Street and Maxwell Street (still familiarly the Poly from Anderson's Polytechnic, the department store previously on the site). Interior rebuilt with fashionable escalator atrium 1988. **Dolcis** occupies the former St Enoch Picture Theatre, remodelled to its present twin-towered form by George A Boswell in 1912. The **Clydesdale Bank**, 163-165 Argyle Street, 1934, by Baird & Thomson, is Art Deco classical with metal spandrelled windows set in strips of rustication.

18 Argyle Street, 1929, James Munro
The original Marks & Spencer store has a certain Art Deco elegance, rather in the manner of Wallis

C McKean

Left Virginia Street. *Below* the ill-fated City of Glasgow Bank whose Glassford Street frontage by James Sellars, 1877-8, was left incomplete on the Bank's failure.

Gilbert's Hoover factory; the giant-arched Italianate **26-34** by James Thomson, 1873, has sadly lost its great cornice.

70-76 Argyle Street approximately reproduces the early 19th-century corner it replaced. The opposite corner, **76-8**, one of the finest remaining c. 1800 blocks in the city, was replaced by the present ingenious design in red sandstone, pyramid-roofed at the corner, by Scott Brownrigg & Turner, 1986-7.

Virginia Street

Named after *the most stately mansion in the whole of the City*, the Virginia Mansion of Alexander Spiers of Elderslie, erected by Provost Buchanan in emulation of the neighbouring Shawfield Mansion in 1756. In its name, scale, privacy and in the use of its buildings, this street recalls—more than anywhere else in Glasgow—the Tobacco Lords, their wealth and their operations. Cleaning and beneficial re-use might have a more dramatic effect in Virginia Street than almost anywhere else in the Merchant City. The Virginia Mansion was designed to close the vista of the new street, and in 1841 that function was taken on by the new **Union Bank**, by David Hamilton which replaced (or converted) the mansion. What can now be seen is a single-storey, domed hall by James Salmon, 1853, with French details and some sculpture.

32 **Virginia Buildings**, 53 Virginia Street, 1817 style of David Hamilton

These balustraded buildings, with Virginia Court behind, comprise some of the best second-generation architecture surviving in the street. Note the large, flat-detailed Venetian window and the fine Ionic double pilasters to the entrances. The douce, 1795 pedimented gable of **No 52** faces the street, with string courses and quoins. Turnpike stair visible in court to rear: an excellent candidate for restoration.

D Walker

Virginia Street was the scene of the City of Glasgow Bank failure in 1878. The worst commercial disaster in the City's history, it was caused by imprudent and illegal activity by the Directors; but as an unlimited company, call could be made upon shareholders. Founded in 1838, it had expanded to 133 branches and was paying a prosperous dividend of 12%. However, in autumn 1878, rumours about possible insolvency grew, and on 2 October it stopped payment. The first call upon shareholders was for 500%, which ruined most; the second call for 2250% brought about unexampled bankruptcy which sucked in many businesses wholly unconnected with the Bank. The street was, for days, the scene of public misery and funereal gloom.

Above Stirling's Library. *Top right* 42 Miller Street, the last survivor of the original villas as drawn by David Small a hundred years ago. *Right* the demolished Venetian Warehouse by Alexander Kirkland at Nos 37-51. *Bottom right* Virginia Buildings, Virginia Street.

Crown Arcade, 31-35 Virginia Street, from 1819
First the Tobacco and then Sugar Exchange, it
retains its galleried interior. **No 31** is now occupied
by the Virginia Galleries, whilst **No 35** has coupled
Corinthian pilasters—a mid 19th-century timber
embellishment. Only the fixing holes remain for the
timber architraves and pediments of the upper
storeys.

Gas Office, 1867, William Leiper and R G Melvin
Now incorporated into Marks & Spencer, this glitzy
intruder is a full flush Italianate palazzo: note its
veritably encrusted doorway, Doric columned and
pedimented first-floor windows, plain attic and rich
cornice above.

Miller Street, from 1761
Originally a street of detached villas, Miller Street
was progressively redeveloped as textile and clothing
warehouses and factories of astonishing grandeur.
Those at its southern end, comprising Clarke &
Bell's 1860 Water Office, David & James Hamilton's
idiosyncratic Western Bank, 1840-1, and—most
tragically of all—Alexander Kirkland's amazing
Venetian courtyard palazzo at **Nos 37-51**, 1854, were
engulfed by later store development facing Argyle
Street.

42 Miller Street, 1775, John Craig
The last survivor of the original villas (along with 52
Charlotte Street, one of the last two survivors of its
type in the Merchant City), built by Craig for
himself. Pedimented, with a Corinthian pilastered
door, it lost its urns and its steep pitched roof
c.1890; its wings had gone even earlier. Fragments
only of the interior remain.

33 **48-56 Miller Street** (former Stirling's Library),
1863, James Smith with J Moyr Smith
A miniature palazzo on the site of Walter Stirling's
villa, built to house the library he bequeathed to the
city in 1791. Note the channelled ground floor,
carved keystones, and beautifully carved chimney.
The library hall remains substantially intact although
its books have long since departed to the Royal
Exchange. **84-92**, c.1877, presumably by Robert
Turnbull, is a late restatement of Alexander
Thomson's motifs lacking in the subtlety it would
have had, had it been built in Thomson's lifetime.

94-104 Miller Street, c.1870s
A Renaissance block breaking into Corinthian
pilasters at the French pavilion-roofed corner.
Interior decoration, furniture and fittings from

Miller Street is narrow as a result
of avarice. John Miller of
Westerton, a superior maltman,
had built himself a villa facing
Argyle Street in 1754, and wished
to profit from rising land values by
feuing his garden into a new street
in 1761. His surveyor, James
Barry, proposed to demolish the
new house. He rejected that on the
grounds of needless extravagance,
and demolished only half,
continuing to live in the other half.
The street was therefore never
other than narrow. The feu
conditions ensured a high-quality
development: *24 self-contained
gentlemen's houses, each house to
consist of a half sunk and 2 square
storeys, but nothing higher. No gable
chimneys or corbie-steps to face the
street. The houses are to be entered
by front doors and a flight of steps
projected on the intended pavement.
No shops and no businesses
disagreeable to Mr Miller.*

Charles Rennie Mackintosh's Ingram Street Tea Rooms on this site remain in the care of Glasgow's Art Galleries and Museums awaiting reassembly.

53-59 Miller Street, 1874
Its architect was at great pains to invert almost every academic canon: since he wisely either did not send his design to the architectural journals, or had his design rejected by every editor, we do not know who he was. A Glaswegian version of architectural goulash.

61-63 Miller Street, 1854, John Burnet (sen)
Italianate with paired central windows and a Romanesque top-floor arcade; more notable internally with a top-lit, galleried well, the balustrading of which has cantilevered shelving for examination of its wares in good light. The arched, laminated trussed roof reflects Burnet senior's particular interest in woodwork. Now converted to flats by John Drummond & Partners.

81 Miller Street, 1849-50, James Salmon
The finest surviving textile warehouse in Glasgow: a Renaissance design of supreme refinement, windows dignified by architraves and occasional conch pediments. Arcaded parapet and original crown glass sash windows. Its sophistication is due to the original client being the coach builder Archibald McLellan, the great art collector.

Above 81 Miller Street. *Below* William Simpson's drawing of Argyle Street, copied from a 1797 original — demonstrating the three ages of Glasgow buildings: crowstepped thatched houses, Palladian villas, and plain later 18th-century tenements.

Anne Dick

Simpson/Mitchell Library

34 **Argyle Arcade**, 1827, John Baird:
98-102 Argyle Street / 28-32 Buchanan Street
The earliest shopping arcade in Scotland, with little in common with its arched and domed London predecessors. Its functional simplicity has rather more in common with the early Parisian arcades (although the nearest parallel to its plain, pilastered iron and timber internal construction is the much larger, contemporary Weybosset Arcade at Providence, Rhode Island). Baird's use of a hammer-beam roof with iron-tie bars appears to be unique among arcades. Now mostly jewellers' shops, but opening off it is the richly Edwardian hostelry of Sloan's

Restaurant (originally the Arcade Café), the facilities of which then included a cigar and tobacco divan, now marred by continuous Muzak.

Crown Tea Rooms, 106-114 Argyle Street,
1770, later remodelled
A wedding present in 1892 from Major John Cochrane to his bride, Miss Catherine Cranston, which she asked David Barclay to remodel into the Crown Lunch and Tea Rooms, in 1895. The interior was entrusted to George Walton (who probably also had a hand in the exterior) and the furnishing, all in oak, to C R Mackintosh. Harled, with quirky detail at the windows, the building had a huge projecting eaves broken by curvilinear gables, the western spectacularly bargeboarded with a pretty oriel. Interesting door with original woodwork, the turnpike stair to the rear; but of Walton's woodwork and pretty stencilling of 1897, and of Mackintosh's basement Dutch Kitchen of 1906, nothing remains visible.

116-120 Argyle Street, 1872-3, William Spence
Once formed part of the right-angled Arthur's & Fraser's (latterly Frasers Sons) department store, extending through to 10-12 Buchanan Street. Sculptured head key-stones by A Macfarlane Shannan pick up the theme of the original Tontine Faces, carved face keystones re-used from the piazza of the Town Hall (see p. 57) on the Buchanan Street frontage.

134-156 Argyle Street, 1900-3, H K Bromhead
Towering, corner-domed Renaissance pile occupying the complete frontage between Buchanan Street and Mitchell Street, built for the warehousemen Stewart and Macdonald (inevitably identified by Glaswegians with the big-kneed and bearded statues of the doorpiece). Its Corinthian order is a continuation of 21-31 Buchanan Street. J H Craigie's turn-of-the-century English neo-Jacobean pub, Da Vinci's, is sadly simplified after a recent fire.

217-221 Argyle Street, 1863, James Thomson
A cast-iron building by the successor to John Baird, (whom he had probably assisted with the pioneer iron building at 36 Jamaica Street), disguised by slim Italianate arcades capped by a massive bracketed cornice. Ironwork, as at Jamaica Street, by R McConnel.

Highlandman's Umbrella, 1901-6, James Miller
Also known as the Central station viaduct, now beautifully restored and repainted. Note the richly ornamental iron pilasters, and tall multi-paned, classical windows.

Above Arthur's Warehouse, corner of Miller and Ingram Streets, by James Boucher, 1875. *Below* Argyle Arcade.

69

Swan/McKean

Ingram Street looking west in the 1820s: Ramshorn Kirk on the right, Hutchesons' Hall tower in the distance, and the Cunninghame Mansion (not yet encased in the Royal Exchange), almost — but not quite — terminating the view at the end.

Everything was rebuilding in late 18th-century Glasgow: a new Trades House (1791): Assembly Rooms (1796), Surgeons' Hall in St Enoch Square (1791), Grammar School (1788), Anderson's Institution (1795), Markets (1790), and new Squares—St Andrew's Square (1787), St Enoch's Square (1782), George Square (1786) and the proposed Stirling's Square (1793); new Professors' Lodgings (1793) and a new Infirmary (1792). Only Charlotte Street, St Andrew's Square and, later, Monteith Row bucked the westward trend. Fashionable Glasgow was moving distinctly north and west.

THE NEW TOWN (or Merchant City)

In 1798, Town Clerk James Denholm could boast of '*the new-built streets to the north of the Trongate called the New Town*'. Glasgow was moving into its fourth important phase of development in the last three decades of the 18th century. It was getting *smart*. The earlier developments and buildings along the Trongate comprised sporadic layout of streets with the detached, often self-indulgent houses of the Virginia merchants. The New Town was the product of the period after the American War of Independence. Tobacco Lords gave way to **King Cotton**—so much so that by 1820, the Merchant City between Candleriggs and Miller Street was occupied largely by the textile industry. Glasgow's New Town differed in investment and control from Edinburgh's. Edinburgh's was a civic project to a competition-winning master-plan. In Glasgow (apart from the abortive laying out of Candleriggs and neighbourhood by the Town Council) the development was undertaken piecemeal, by private entrepreneurs. Existing routes, or the new streets opening backwards from the Trongate, were used as determinants, with all their limitations.

In 1786, construction of the New Town began with generally large, four-storey blocks of shops and warehouses, with residential accommodation above, in Albion Street, Queen Street, Ingram Street and George Street. The premier developer was the Glasgow Buildings Company, founded by Dugald Bannatyne, John Thomson and Robert Smith. The same trio then followed with a further phase of Brunswick, Wilson, John, and Hutcheson Streets in 1790.

The streets were laid out in a Beaux-Arts manner with major edifices facing down streets closing the vistas: Ingram Street by the magnificent portico of the Royal Exchange; the Candleriggs by the Ramshorn Kirk, Glassford Street by the Star Inn, Hutcheson Street by the new Hospital, Virginia Street by the Virginia Mansion, George Street by St George's Tron Kirk, Buchanan Street by St Enoch's Kirk and Garth Street by the Trades House at one end, and the Merchants' House at the other.

Ingram Street
The spine of the New Town, originally closed to the High Street, and terminated to the west by the Royal Exchange to which it runs *'straight as a sunbeam... and at its furthest extremity is terminated by a very handsome building with an open court and wings adorned with all the ornament that the Grecian architecture can bestow'*. The handsome building was the mansion of Cunninghame of Lainshaw in Queen Street, now reclothed as the Royal Exchange (see p. 88). A spacious, broad concourse, it was graced with important civic monuments: the Ramshorn Kirk, the Athenaeum, Hutchesons' Hospital, the Star Inn, the New County Buildings, some good banks, and the Royal Exchange.

35 **St David's (Ramshorn) Kirk,** 98 Ingram Street, 1824, Thomas Rickman
The English architect who first classified medieval church architecture into styles, Rickman was employed to replace an unfashionable 18th-century God box; which he did in academic Early Decorated, in a squeezed, vertically proportioned cruciform building. Town Superintendent James Cleland inserted the crypt and altered the staircase, making the church stand higher than originally intended. The principal mercantile memorials to Glasgow are divided between this spooky graveyard (built originally upon the cherry and apple trees, gooseberry and currant bushes, kaill, leeks and other ground herbs belonging to Hutchesons' Hospital) and the Necropolis. The original burying ground was clipped severely when laying out the widened Ingram Street. (Colour plate, p. 82)

As a residential quarter, the New Town lasted barely two decades. Fashionable merchants were sucked west by the fine houses on Blythswood Hill, beginning a long trek west, which only ended in Bearsden at the turn of the 20th century. Banks, markets and warehouses—and, above all, the cotton industry—swarmed into these houses from as early as 1820. By 1840, it had become very similar in composition to London's Covent Garden. By mid-century, the financial heart of the City followed the commercial heart of the city west, leaving the New Town behind. It became the wholesale area, increasingly neglected and under threat of post-war redevelopment to higher densities. The return of Glasgow's concert hall to the Candleriggs was the first tentative step in a process that has made the area now one of the most vibrant in the city.

Dr James Cleland, 1770-1840
A wright and builder with an enquiring and scientific mind. Having first of all been on the Town Council he decided that it would perhaps be best if he ran the city himself and in 1814 secured the appointment of Superintendent of Public Works. In 1819, he took a census of the population, the first ever taken in the United Kingdom, earning him an LLD from the University of Glasgow in 1826. He was a prolific writer, notably *Annals of Glasgow* (1816) and *An Historical Account of the Bills of Mortality, and the Probability of Human Life in Glasgow and Other Large Towns* (1836). He designed the Old Post Office in Nelson Street, 1810, dem.1840; the Magdalen Asylum, 1812; the Bazaar, since much reconstructed, 1817; and the Old High School in Upper Montrose Street, 1820.

Above R W Billings's design for Ingram Street warehouses (now Ingram Square). *Right* Ingram Square, corner Brunswick and Wilson Street. *Below* Old Hutchesons' Hospital.

Hutchesons' Hospital was founded 1639-41 by George Hutcheson of Lambhill and his brother Thomas, both lawyers, for 12 old men and 12 boys, with a building facing the Trongate. In the Glasgow style of this period. it consisted of a two-storey block, principal rooms on the first floor, a steeple, and an L-block stretching out behind with circular stair towers. The expansion of Glasgow westwards gave the Hospital a chance to realise the asset of the building and garden by feueing a street, and using the capital to build a new hall, in the fashion of the time.

Ingram Square, from 1982, Elder & Cannon
The name given to the entire block between the Candleriggs and Brunswick Street. A variety of older houses and warehouses are knit together with an outstanding new one to form a square of flats and shops. The Candleriggs corner is occupied by **Descartes**, a steel-framed inter-war warehouse with characteristic large-paned windows. The rest of the Ingram Street frontage, and most of upper Brunswick Street, is occupied by the fascinating 1854 façades by R W Billings. Billings's books *Baronial and Ecclesiastical Antiquities of Scotland* were primarily

responsible for the Victorian Baronial revival, although here he eschewed revivalism himself. His crisp, finely detailed and eccentric façades owe little to historic Scots precedent: Dutch gables, reinterpreted turrets, oriel windows and string courses are pure invention. Indeed, his building further down **Brunswick Street**, with its aversion to any right angle, could almost be said to presage the buildings of Rudolph Steiner.

Below David Hamilton's original drawing for Hutchesons' Hospital. *Left* the view up Hutcheson Street.

Hunterian Museum

C. McKean

36 **Hutchesons' Hall,** Ingram Street, 1802, David Hamilton

In this splendid, delicate—almost French—design (modified internally by John Baird II in 1876), the young Hamilton gave clear notice of his future stature as one of Glasgow's greatest architects. The principal storey is recessed behind Corinthian columns, and flanked by bays containing statues of James Hutcheson and George Hutcheson carved in 1655 by James Colquhoun (who, as well as being an artist, invented Glasgow's first fire engine, and ended up a Bailie.) The attic is decorated with sculpture and a balustrade, and the tower proceeds gracefully from square, to drum, to conical as it gets higher. Smaller rooms and offices on the ground floor, fine staircase to piano nobile or principal floor and Baird's hall, with its huge windows, wonderfully idiosyncratic pediments, and rich plasterwork. Good ironwork. Converted by Jack Notman to the West of Scotland HQ for the National Trust for Scotland. **Open to the public: shop**. (Colour plate, p. 83)

The Star Inn and its Host, Henry Hemmings, once earned itself a couplet from Glasgow's McGonagall, Blind Alick (Alexander MacDonald 1771-1830).

'And first they gave me brandy,
And then they gave me gin;
Here's long life to the worthy waiters
Of Mr Hemmings' Hotel and Inn'.

Alick had arrived at the Trongate from England in 1790, and soon established himself as Glasgow's wandering minstrel, being appropriately married in the *Whistlin' Kirkie*. The city's perpetual desire for status led to his designation the '*Glasgow Homer*', to which he responded with the truly majestic strophes:

'I've travelled all the world over,
And many a place beside;
But I never saw a more beautiful
City
Than that on the navigable river, the
Clyde.'

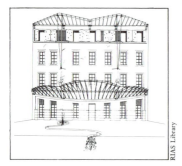

RIAS Library

Anne Dick

RCAHMS

Former Bank of Scotland, 176 Ingram Street, 1828, William Burn
Centrepiece of the block between John and South Frederick Streets, one of the best surviving in the entire street. Replacing the blousy Star Inn in 1828 as the focus of the vista up Glassford Street, this dignified bank forms a symmetrical composition framed by slightly advanced wings framed (almost boxed) by pilasters sitting on a plinth of channelled stonework. Under restoration by Page & Park as the Italian Centre.

Assembly Rooms (demolished), 1796, James Adam
The Adam design rose to the stylistic challenge required by Assembly rooms, card, supper and retiring rooms, erected by public subscription. The Ionic Triumphal Arch which dominated the façade beneath its balustraded parapet was re-erected as MacLennan Arch in Glasgow Green (see p. 33). Wings by Henry Holland. Its **Post Office** replacement, begun by W T Oldrieve, 1889, is huge and Italianate.

TSB West of Scotland HQ, 1866, John Burnet, 1894-1900, Sir J J Burnet
Son extended father's plain, three-storeyed Italianate bank with a galleried upper storey, and a jewel-like, domed banking hall in front, of such personality as to reduce his father's building to relative insignificance. Apart from the dome with its cupola, note particularly the beautifully carved cartouches within the broken pediments above the windows, and the composition of the main entrance in which a diminutive pediment on wriggly columns surges through the pediment above: modelled from a doorway in St Mary's Oxford, with sculpture by Sir George Frampton. It seems to presage *fin-de-siècle*, although the interior is still a pure example of Beaux-Arts taste.

Lanarkshire House, 191 Ingram Street, 1876-9
A John Burnet refacing of David Hamilton's 1841 former Union Bank, which replaced the Virginia Mansion facing down Virginia Street. Lavishly Italianate: boldly corniced and pedimented entrance into rusticated plinth: two principal floors whose granite-shafted columns flank wide (windows) and narrow (solid) bays. Statues by John Mossman at second-floor level beneath a voracious cornice and balustrade above. Interior transformed into courts, although the good 1853 banking hall by James Salmon (sen) is recoverable.

Mitchell Library

Wilson Street

The heart of the Merchant City: really a plaza, enclosed on all sides, and originally given a homogeneity by its flat-detailed New Town architecture. Despite great changes, it is still magnificent to be in. The north eastern block, once occupied by a survivor of the New Town with its flat details, Venetian windows and pilasters, is now occupied by the most adventurous modern component of **Ingram Square** by Elder & Cannon. The corner is turned by a patterned brick and glass drum protruding above the roofline, the remainder of the street being completed with a classically-based Post-Modern colourful extravaganza.

37 **County Buildings**, 40-50 Wilson Street, 1844, Clarke & Bell
Beginning at the south end as a competition-winning scheme for City and County Buildings, and later extended north for the Merchants' House, and—in 1871—right the way up to Ingram Street for the City. After the construction of the City Chambers in George Square, it became a Sheriff Court with cells of legendary odour. It is a massive building, its south side dominated by a giant Ionic columned portico astride a plinth (but not a genuine portico since there is no entrance into it). The centre of the west façade is the 10 Corinthian-columned façade to the former Merchants' House, in very graceful neo-Greek, designed to face the Trades House down Garth Street. Currently under plans for conversion to a Fashion Centre by Building Design Partnership.

The heart of the Merchant City from the corner of Hutcheson Street: note Hutchesons' Hall, the arcaded buildings on the right, and the shallow, flat-relief classical details that distinguished Glasgow New Town architecture.

TSB Booking Hall by J J Burnet.

RIAS Library

Mitchell Library

Above the Merhants' House, facing down Garth Street.

Glasgow Herald Building.

C. McKean

Links House, on the corner of Brunswick Street, is another tall, steel-framed, red stone commercial tower by J Taylor Thomson, 1932.

60 Wilson Street, c.1792, probably Robert Smith
The most complete surviving block of the original New Town, its appearance much altered by paintwork, poor windows and a mutilating roof. The rusticated, arcaded ground floor was probably originally open. Details above include flat, twinned pilasters, blind arched windows, and thermal windows capping the flanking bays, all seeking to impart the kind of dignity to this building that obtains in Great King Street, Edinburgh.

76-84 Wilson Street, 1889, Alexander Skirving
Very ornate: arches upon giant Ionic columns, pilasters, and much sculptured and incised ornament—blending Alexander Thomson with 1880s French—the latter trend exemplified by a pointed dome, since replaced.

38**Glasgow Herald Building** Albion Street, 1936, Sir E Owen Williams
A fine office and printing works of horizontal strips of opaque black and clear glass, built originally for the *Daily Express*, and a brother to that in Fleet Street. Its façade is a pure curtain-wall of glass and black vitrolite panels, the load being carried by the framed structure within. **Nos 131-141 Albion Street**

Above and left John Street Church.

is a reasonably adventurous, steel-framed modern warehouse of 1906 by H E Clifford. The 1986 extension to the Albion St newspaper offices on the corner of **George Street**, by Frank Burnet, Bell, fails to maintain the scale, and substitutes low, curved, blue and grey moulded shapes in high-tech aesthetic for the black and white curtain wall of 50 years earlier.

John Street

Named thus after the extraordinary number of Glaswegian bigwigs who bore that Christian name, it opened with the (demolished) new market required for New Town residents and the original **Anderson's Institution:** designed by Robert Smith in 1795: a hemispherical hall seating 500, a library, laboratories and committee rooms. **Nos 9-17** c.1840 comprise a good row of the second generation commercial offices to invade the Merchant City.

39 **John Street Church**, 1859-60, J T Rochead
Sitting upon and entered through a hugely rusticated plinth of deep channelled stonework, the double-height principal floor presents a virtual curtain-wall of glass. The glazing is fixed directly into an Ionic colonnade, with boldly swagged capitals, framed by a solid bay at each corner, with a giant, elegantly carved niche. Masculine cornice and balustrade above. Wondrously rich ceiling within obscured by conversion into a restaurant.

Robert Smith's original plan for the **New Town** was to extend Bell Street due west as a primary artery. It was frustrated by a Dr Scruton (who had had to be bribed north to teach at Hutchesons') who refused to sell his house in Candleriggs. If you look along Bell Street from the High Street into the flank of some original Candleriggs warehouses, the consequent constipation becomes evident. Smith dog-legged his route inconveniently north, forming Wilson Street (named after a charity school), whose westward progress was now blocked by the Tobacco Lord mansion of John Bowman of Ashgrove. That house was replaced in 1814 by Virginia Buildings (see p. 65).

Original building for the Andersonian Institution, George Street, with first section of the Royal College on the right.

City Chambers' extension.

Mitchell Library

Watson, Salmond & Gray

GEORGE STREET

Of '*the finest street in the New Town*' nothing original survives east of George Square: the north side much colonised in concrete by Strathclyde University, and the south anticipating its fourth-generation redevelopment.

Montrose House, 187 George Street, 1939, Stewart Sim
Delayed by the Second World War and constructed in the 1950s, the corner to Montrose Street is turned with a circular glazed drum, and a frigid echo of 1930s details. **23 Montrose Street** is unfriendly Victorian, 1894, by A B MacDonald, with pedimented corner tower, Venetian windows and petrified baroque details.The scale of the street now is better exemplified by the huge 1876 warehouse with its Renaissance details at **No 18**, now converted into flats with its central arched bays hollowed out into attractive balconies; or by the more pleasing Jacobean-style warehouse and office by James Thomson,1898, at **Nos 10-12**.

On the site of the **Grammar School**, 1788, by John Craig, towers the competition-winning giant, red stone Italianate **Royal College of Science and Technology**, 1901-9, by David Barclay, now part of Strathclyde University (see p. 21).

266 George Street, 1900-2, Thomson & Sandilands
Former Parish Council offices inflating Baroque to proportions never originally intended: domed centrepiece recessed between pavilion-roofed towers, giant Ionic order with Doric entablature (a Beaux-Arts conceit) emerging from canted oriel windows and entered through a granite-columned doorpiece. **No 280**, adjacent, was designed in 1885 by W W Robertson, in pleasant Italian, as the Income Tax Office. Cast-iron Corinthian columns within.

City Chambers extension, 1913, Watson, Salmond & Gray
Academically correct francophile block linked across John Street to the main Chambers by superb, French triumphal arches with paired Ionic columns and urns. Its eastern neighbour, **291-229 George Street** by Ian Burke & Partners, 1986, is an office block which derives its proportions from these grander earlier buildings, maintaining an appropriate scale and rhythm.

Above unrealised scheme by Robert and James Adam for a block on the south side of George Square. *Left* George Square looking east in the 1870s: a pleasant classical square, but never as grand as the Adams would have wished.

⁴⁰**George Square**, from 1786

Originally a low-density square of three-storey houses with a private fenced garden in the middle, which always lacked the palace-front grandeur that ensured the survival of contemporary squares elsewhere. It nearly happened: in 1792, Robert and James Adam prepared a plan for the south side: two houses with warehouses between South Frederick Street and Hanover Street for John Maire, and a much grander block seemingly for the entire south side for Messrs Todd & Shortridge. It is probable that the slow sale and near bankruptcy of Bannatyne and his colleagues prevented its realisation. To judge by its almost provincial scale, the east side reflected their fright; the north side was not begun until c.1807 by which date confidence had returned.

The Square was soon colonised by hotels, its status damaged by the arrival of the railway. By 1850, it had become wholly mercantile. The gardens in the middle gave place to lamp standards and statues to Scots worthies like Burns, Scott and Glasgow's local hero Sir John Moore of Corunna. J T Rochead planned an elegantly classical single-storey market for the entire Square somewhat in the manner of Covent Garden, but nothing transpired. Instead the Square has become the focus of ceremonial, symbolic and political Glasgow.

Copthorne Hotel, from 1807

Remodelled survivor of the original Square, yet—despite the lumpy roof (1903), paint, and billowing new conservatory—retaining the original thin Georgian details and unconvincing pilasters, characteristic of Glaswegian classicism of this period.

Detail of another unbuilt Adam block for George Square.

Anne Dick

Right and below City Chambers now and
as originally drawn.

RIAS Library

41**City Chambers**, 1883-8, William Young
Grandiose competition winner by a London Scot who
sought to bring Venice to Glasgow (and restore
confidence to the city after the City of Glasgow Bank
crash). Three tiers of paired classical columns
support a pediment, itself flanked by miniature
turrets. Each corner carries a domed cupola, and the
entire composition is dominated by a surprisingly
modern tower, also capped by a cupola. A wealth of
carving by George Lawson and others around the
entrance. The interior is even more lavish than the
façade—particularly the glowing galleries and marbled
staircases which flank the mosaic basilica of the
entrance hall (Colour plate, p. 81). The arched and
columned Banqueting Hall contains decoration by
such Glasgow Boys as Henry, Lavery, Roche and
Walton.

The south-east block of George Square is occupied
by the **General Post Office**, 1875-6, by Robert
Mathieson, and later extended down to Ingram
Street. Graceful Italianate whose channelled
stonework, segmental windowheads, architraves,
balustraded aprons etc lend dignity and proportion to
the façade, its profile was altered when the end bays
were raised.

Right the Merchants' House and the City Chambers painted by Antony Alexander. *Below* one of the great staircases in the City Chambers.

H

Top left the Ramshorn Kirk. *Top* the Trongate, looking east in the early 19th century. *Above* painting by Sam Bough of a proposal by J T Rochead for a classical market in the centre of George Square in the manner of Covent Garden. *Left* Royal Bank, Glassford Street.

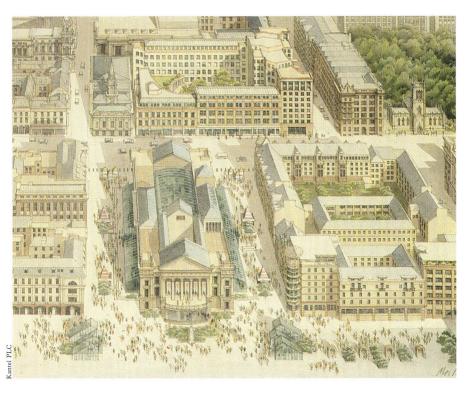

Aerial perspective by Kantel of the Merchant City: *right to left* Ramshorn Kirk, Cochrane Square, Hutchesons' Hall, and the Italian Centre. *Far top left* City Chambers. *Centre* the Sheriff Court soon to become a Fashion Centre. *Centre left* one of the few surviving blocks of the New Town. *Centre right* Ingram Square.

Below the Clydesdale Banking Hall, St Vincent Place. *Below left* Hutcheson's Hall.

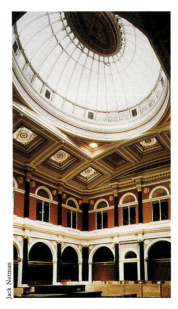

Above the interior of Princes Square.
Right the interior of Stirling's Library.

Hugh Martin & Partners

Anne Dick

RCAHMS

5 Hanover Street, 1923, James Miller
Only half of the full George Square frontage of this
fine, American-classical building was ever completed,
probably designed by Miller's American-influenced
assistant, Richard Gunn.

George Square west side was developed
originally as a three-storey terrace of houses,
pedimented in the middle. It had become occupied
by hotels, eg Clarence, Crow, Globe, Waverley, by
1800, and in 1869, the Bank of Scotland rebuilt the
Waverley and a section of St Vincent Place, as their
Glasgow head office (*see* St Vincent Place) to designs
by J T Rochead. The **Bank of Scotland** rebuilt the
central section in 1874, by James Sellars following
Rochead's lead. John Burnet's northern third for the
Merchants' House also reproduced Rochead's
detailing exactly, to produce a composition which
was an extruded version of the Bank.

42 **Merchants' House,** 1874-7, John Burnet
Entered from West George Street, richly detailed
with Corinthian oriel windows at its corner bays, its
domed tower bears a merchant ship in full sail, as
had the original Merchants' Steeple in the Briggait.
In 1907, the younger Burnet added a further two
storeys to increase the rented office element, skilfully
concealed behind giant columns.

RCAHMS

Top the west side of George Square, its
Italianate symmetry destroyed by the
upper floors of the Merchants' House
on the right. *Above* Merchants' Hall.

QUEEN STREET

151-155 Queen Street.

Queen Street and Royal Exchange Square

The ancient thoroughfare of Cow Loan only became Queen Street after James Barry causewayed it at a regular width of 55 ft. It was flanked by generously proportioned plots for large mercantile villas, which had a very short life. Redevelopment, mainly of four-storeyed tenements and warehouses, began in the early 19th century, a second wave at the turn of the present century; and a third in the 1960s, when it lost many of its best buildings, including David Hamilton's 1840 Clydesdale Bank (Nos 11-13) and British Linen Bank (No 110); James Wylson's Canada Court (Nos 78-82), and John Baird's 1854 MacDonald Sewed Muslin Warehouses (Nos 120-134). 21-41 on the west side now best exemplifies the early re-development of the street.

Anne Dick

David Hamilton (1768-1843) was one of Glasgow's finest architects, and dominated the city in the early 19th century with a series of public buildings, and delightful suburban mansions for the mercantile gentry, much in the manner of Sir John Soane. Son of a mason (possibly the designer of St Andrew Square), his first major building was Hutchesons' Hospital (1802) which he followed with the Theatre Royal, Royal Exchange, Normal School, several banks, the Western Club, numerous churches including St Enoch's (now demolished) and works to almost 30 country houses including major additions to Hamilton Palace. Dr John Strang considered: '*Perhaps no one has contributed more to the architectural adornment of Glasgow than that gifted and tasteful individual.... Like most men of genius, he possessed great modesty, and kind and convivial habits endeared himself to a large circle of attached friends, who valued his talents and bewailed his loss.*'

Guild Hall, 45-67 Queen Street,
1899, David Barclay

Reticulated, red-sandstone pile, iron- and steel-framed with arched, hollow tile floors. Built as Hunter Barr's warehouse, it is now offices, with a huge white-walled atrium by Covell Matthews at its middle. Its grandiloquent mahogany and marble entrance was most sensibly retained. John Gibson's superb 1847 National Bank and Stock Exchange formerly on this site survives in exile as Langside Hall at Queen's Park. Opposite **Nos 30-44**, by Thomson & Sandilands, 1912, another tall red sandstone block with canted bays recessed between Greek Ionic columns.

Charlotte House, 78-82 Queen Street,
1968, John Drummond

Five storeys of aggregate panels surmounted by a repetitive tower block. It replaced James Wylson's 1845 Canada Court, singled out by Henry-Russell Hitchcock as Glasgow's representative warehouse in *Early Victorian Architecture in Britain.*

South and Royal Exchange Courts,
73-77 Queen Street, 1830, Robert Black

Entered through a tall severe block, with a curious niched and balustraded parapet, they comprise two three-storey mercantile business chambers. Pioneer examples of their kind, both have Black's characteristic channelled stone ground floors, with segment-headed windows. The South Court has consoled doorways, while those of Royal Exchange Court are dignified by pilasters.

Queen Court, 54-72 Queen Street, c.1833
The only survivor of Queen Street's several warehouse courts, notable for its long classical façade of regularly spaced windows.

151-155 Queen Street, 1834, David Hamilton
Business chambers for the connoisseur businessman Archibald McLellan. One of Hamilton's finest designs, with Corinthian pilasters, and a subsidiary pilastrade threaded through it, as at the Exchange and its Square; a superbly sculptured frieze and an attic in the manner of Sir John Soane. McLellan's building contains a lozenge-plan stair, cantilevered landings stayed from the roof on suspension rods.

The former **Arthur's Warehouse** has a curving mullioned façade by James Manson of Miller & Manson, 1947-50, a rebuilding of James Boucher's extension of Canada Court after war damage; extensive refurbishment, new ground floor and new storey on roof, 1988-9, by John Drummond & Partners. The **Bank of Scotland** was a competition win by T P Bennet & Son, built in 1972 after David Hamilton's Mannerist bank, overloaded with Venetian additional floors, developed structural problems.

136-148 Queen Street, 1902, James Miller
Like so many American office blocks of that time, one building seemingly built on top of another. The upper one, defined by a cantilevered balcony, has a Doric colonnade.

43**Royal Exchange Square**, from 1827, Archibald Elliot II, David Hamilton and Robert Black
Nothing quite like Exchange Square exists elsewhere in Europe. The idea derived, perhaps, from reconstructions of the Forum of Augustus, a parallel which must have seemed more significant when the Exchange was the city's commercial heart. Like St Andrew's Square, it is of that peculiarly Glasgow form, a square with a building occupying the central area. The building, as usual, arrived first—in 1778, when William Cunninghame of Lainshaw built a fine Tobacco Lord's house in a large garden. It was bought in 1817 by the Royal Bank which, in 1827, commissioned Archibald Elliot II to prepare plans for a new bank to the rear and terraces of shops and business chambers to north and south. The mansion and the remaining land in the centre of the square were then sold to the New Exchange Committee.

Royal Exchange Square. *Below*, in 1834.

The detailed authorship of the Exchange Square is unclear. Elliot was described as its architect, and its elevations must be broadly his. The panelled shop pilasters, however, and the first-floor pilastrades threaded through the giant order are distinctly like Hamilton's. David Hamilton and his son-in-law James Smith (*father of Madeleine*, see p. 118) certainly built the north side in 1830-9, an onerous undertaking which seems to have contributed to the sequestration of their property in 1844.

Royal Exchange.

Anne Dick

Royal Exchange (Stirling's Library),
from 1827, David Hamilton
The Cunninghame mansion refaced with giant
pilasters, fronted by a huge portico of Corinthian
columns supporting a cupola above—proportioned
more to suit the vista down Ingram Street than the
building itself. The mansard, added in 1880, housed
Glasgow's first telephone exchange. The vestibule is
domed and galleried. The elevations of the hall to
the rear are clearly modelled on Sir John Soane's
Bank of England, whereas the 130-ft long coffered
vault inside, carried upon Corinthian columns, is
modelled on the new Signet Library in Edinburgh
(Colour plate, p. 84). For a time, this building was
the *Glasgow Rialto . . . here the heavy news has come
to many an Antonio of the loss of sea-borne Argosies
and to others of mercantile misfortune.* The statue of
Wellington in front of the building was completed by
Baron Marochetti in 1844.

Royal Bank of Scotland, Royal Exchange Square,
1827, Archibald Elliot II
Linked to terraces north and south by triumphal
arches with coupled Ionic columns, the Bank's pure
Greek Ionic exterior, modelled on the Erechtheum in
Athens, remains intact, and gives the Square a close-
built, columnar grandeur. The interior succumbed, in
the 1960s, to the third refashioning in contemporary

RCAHMS

Royal Bank, Royal Exchange Square.
Below St Vincent Place looking east.

taste. Just beyond the arch, the red lobster of
Rogano restaurant, 1937, by Weddell & Inglis
advertises its glitzy *Moderne* presence. The finest
1930s consumer survival, its façade has all the tricks;
chrome, vitrolite in black, yellow, red and silver.

St Vincent Place, from 1835
Unusually spacious rectangular place between George
Square and Buchanan Street, whose original character
can still be interpreted from the huge 1835 four-
storey block **Nos 1-15** on the south side: plainly
classical, architraved windows over shops and
balustraded parapet.

44 **Bank of Scotland, St Vincent Place,**
1869, J T Rochead
Mercantile grandeur in the form of an Italianate
palazzo, its tightly controlled restlessness
characteristic of Rochead. By boldness of scale and
detail, such as the conch-shaped tympana above
ground-floor windows, and pediments above those on
the principal floor, Rochead transforms other
architects' details into his own. Huge carved
doorpiece by William Mossman.

Clydesdale Bank, 30-40 St Vincent Place,
1870, John Burnet
Renaissance façade of coupled and tripled columns,
sitting above a heavily rusticated plinth with round

Anne Dick

Bank of Scotland,
St Vincent Place.

Clydesdale Bank,
St Vincent Place.

headed door and windows, enlivened by carved roundels. Head of Father Clyde over the door, and the figures of Industry and Commerce, by the Mossmans. Glass-roofed two-storey banking hall, the present colour scheme of which is due to Jack Notman (Colour plate, p. 83). *The Bailie's* architectural correspondent considered Burnet to be here *more of a decorator than an architect. He has left the large lines of the magnificent entablature of the Madeira Court Warehouse for petty prettiness of broken pediments, three-quarter columns and mansard roofs.* Three western bays slightly later, c. 1880.

Bank of England (originally Citizen Building), 24 St Vincent Place, 1885-9, T L Watson

An early use of red Dumfriesshire stone in a five-storey composition: sophisticated early Italian Renaissance at entrance level (drawn by the scholar-architect W J Anderson) and northern European Renaissance above, including an arcaded attic storey like Blois. Twin, scroll-crowstepped gables and a corbelled clock turret on the skyline. Carving by James Hendry. The **Anchor Line Building** next door, 1906-7, by James Miller is an early example of that architect's taste for plain white architecture, and skill in cramming seven storeys alongside his neighbour's five. Façade of faience. Excellent Ionic-columned entrance, with delightful cherubs making garlands of seaweed and seashells, modelled by H H Martyn of Cheltenham. The ground-floor office has a deep luscious frieze, marble Ionic columns, and an oak chimney-piece conjuring up the atmosphere of their liners for prospective passengers.

Anchor Line Building, Bank of England clock turret on left.

Scottish Amicable, 31-39 St Vincent Place, 1870-3, Campbell Douglas & Stevenson

Italianate palazzo with Renaissance window details, and central bay emphasised by a Corinthian porch, distorted by Burnet & Boston's addition of upper floors with oriel windows to bring it in line with its neighbours. Sculpture by William Mossman.

Scottish Provident Institute, 17-29 St Vincent Place, 1904-6, J M Dick Peddie

Colossal six-storey and basement office building, squeezed into what should be four storeys; two-storey rusticated plinth, three storeys above flanked by three-bay giant-columned pavilions; cornice, attic, capacious French roofs above the pavilions (to bring total number of storeys within to nine).

Right Buchanan Street in its heyday in 1834: note St Enoch's Church closing the vista at the bottom. *Below* elevation of the bottom part of Buchanan Street in 1842, showing the combination of grand Palladian mansions and merchants' premises.

Swan/McKean

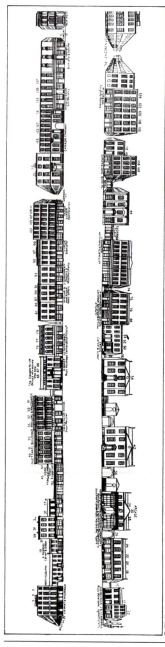

D Walker

BUCHANAN STREET

Glasgow's finest individual street (even if Gordon and Hope Streets and the eastern halves of St Vincent Street and West George Street run it close). Successfully pedestrianised in 1978 to designs by the City Planning Department, it is very different now from 30 years ago, when it was the city's main traffic artery, and home each night to countless thousands of starlings. Begun as a street of mansions, it was completed as three- or four-storey commercial. By 1841, redevelopment had begun in earnest. Great household stores concentrated at the south end and (with the exception of the Art Deco classical extravaganza of Burton's, 1938, by R I Pierce & N Martin), all still date from before 1900.

45 Fraser's, 21-61 Buchanan Street

Fraser's comprises five buildings of which the southern four were Victorian department stores. **21-31**, 1879, Macdonald's, by William Spence, is a design of supreme elegance: Corinthian pilastered at the uppermost floors, retaining its original ground-floor shop windows. **37** was Kemp's shawl emporium, originally a three-storey iron front, built 1853-4 and the earliest of its kind; top floors later. **45** was Wylie & Lochhead's. It may be that William Lochhead, the architect member of the firm, was responsible for the original design: iron colonnades divided into three bays by masonry piers, with a giant Corinthian order. The magnificent four-storey cast-iron saloon with glazed arched roof was rebuilt by James Sellars, 1883, following the latest American theories on structural fire protection. Sellars' galleried saloon is high and spacious, with banded terracotta piers and a magnificent mahogany stair with dolphins at the entrance end. Sellars' façade was more elaborate, with bows in the outer bays and much delicate early Renaissance detail, the entrance pedimented with figures representing Industry and

Buchanan Street commemorates Andrew Buchanan, a maltster turned tobacco merchant, who bought up land on Argyle Street in 1760 and erected a mansion at the south-west corner. In 1773, he built a large houseblock opposite, with an entry between. In 1777 Buchanan feued the land behind the entry into a street, James Johnston taking the first lot, **No 42**, and erecting a handsome pedimented villa with flanking pavilions. Further large pedimented houses were built at **30** and **54**. By 1779, Buchanan's firms had failed as a result of the American War of Independence, and his properties were bought by John & Alexander Gordon, West India Merchants. Buchanan's house was only partially demolished, leaving a bottleneck at the south end which was not eliminated until 1900. Several exceptional houses were built, the finest being the pilastered house at **94**, built in 1804 for Alexander 'Picture' Gordon (the first of Glasgow's art collectors) to house his Italian and Dutch masterpieces; and Robert Dennistoun's at **65-69**, for which he obtained designs from Sir John Soane in 1798.

Art. **49-53**, Mirrlee's, tall five-storeyed Renaissance with pilastered top floor, was originally three-storeys, heightened by Boucher & Cousland. The fifth Fraser building, **55-61**, was built c.1840 for the great lithographic and engraving house of Maclure & Macdonald. The ground floor is elegantly classical with consoled windows and a pierced parapet above.

No 14 on the east side, represents the original Fraser & Sons store, built for Arthur & Fraser by William Spence in 1873, superimposed pilastrades and an arcaded top floor, rebuilt after a bad fire by Baird & Thomson in 1889. It re-used some of the Tontine heads which its builder, James Shannan, had rescued from the City Hall. In **No 20**, built in 1888-9, nominally by John Hutcheson, Andrew Black was assisted by Charles Rennie Mackintosh, to whom the superb quality of the detailing is doubtless due. Argyle Chambers, **28-32**, 1904, by Colin Menzies is a swaggeringly sculptured red sandstone baroque, with gold mosaic semi-domes over the entrance to the arcade. It contained Glasgow Style rooms decorated by McCulloch & Co.

Left Buchanan Street, looking south today. *Below* the south-west section of Buchanan Street.

Prince's Square, 1842, John Baird I
Long three-storey, classical façade, the balustrade replaced in 1987. Within Prince's Square was an old-fashioned court of business chambers, a stable and coach-houses in the middle, much favoured by shipowners, since it backed the original Stock Exchange in Queen Street. In 1986-7, the stable was demolished, the court splendidly roofed and a galleried specialist shopping centre inserted, to designs by Hugh Martin & Partners. The clue to its success is its circulation: banks of escalators, glass lifts, and splendidly baroque stairs, all overlooked by balconies, create a sense of Second Empire opera: customers go as much to see and be seen, as to shop. The ironwork by Dawson Shepley looks like sticks of melted liquorice. (Colour plate, p. 84).

Below Royal Insurance building.
Bottom 63-69 Buchanan Street.

RIAS Library

63-69 Buchanan Street, 1879, James Sellars
Mossman statues of Caxton and Gutenberg between the gables at the top, and carvings of cherubs engaged in journalistic and printing pursuits at the mezzanine, testify to its original purpose as the *Glasgow Herald* office. Otherwise early Renaissance with giant Corinthian columns at the centre bay.
71-79, 1880, giant Corinthian pilastered arcade by James Thomson for those great property speculators, the glass merchants John and Daniel MacDougall.

85 Buchanan Street, 1970, Gillespie Kidd & Coia
Probably Glasgow's most subtle post-war infill building. A narrow frontage block originally for BOAC, clad in copper, which provides the rhythm of, and perfectly complements, its stone-built, vertically proportioned neighbours. Between it and Gordon Street, a run of three original late Georgian buildings interrupted by the Clydesdale Bank, **91**, 1891, built as Miss Cranston's Buchanan Street Tea Rooms to impeccable 'Pont Street Dutch' design in banded stonework and Viennese café ironwork by G Washington Browne.

60-62 Buchanan Street, 1898, Robert Thomson
A slim, seven-storey red sandstone elevator building mixing baroque and that typical *fin-de-siècle* detail of canted bays within arched recesses. Sinuous balconies above give the design plenty of movement. plenty of movement.

64 Buchanan Street, 1851, John Baird I
Distinctive design of German neo-classical derivation, with cast-iron mullioned windows and finely sculptured detail implying the hand of Alexander Thomson. **78-80**, barest classical of c.1835, is the

Mitchell Library

only known building of Robert Foote, the wealthy plasterer-architect whose intervention made Alexander Thomson architect rather than solicitor. The Thomson-like top floor is a slightly later addition.

Royal Bank of Scotland, 1850-1, Charles Wilson
Rear extension to the bank in Royal Exchange Square, replacing Alexander 'Picture' Gordon's mansion. Boldly classical, with architraved windows and a big cornice, richly embellished with finely sculptured detail.

Royal Insurance Building, 106-112 Buchanan Street, 1897-8, Thomson & Sandilands
Competition-winning design in free Renaissance style. Sandilands's Beaux-Arts training in evidence at the fine sculptured detail.

Royal Bank Building, 1887, Sydney Mitchell
Something of a landmark in Glasgow's architecture. This Edinburgh architect introduced the big domed corner, a feature that Glasgow architects were soon to make peculiarly their own. The adjoining **Carron Building (Nos 123-129)** was built by James Boucher as the Glasgow offices of the great Falkirk ironfounders.

St Vincent Chambers, 116-128 Buchanan Street,
1898-1902, Burnet & Boston
A tall, red-sandstone elevator building on a slim, single houseplot frontage to St Vincent Place,

Left 85-91 Buchanan Street. *Below* Mackintosh's unsuccessful design for the National Bank at the corner of St Vincent Street. *Bottom* Royal Bank.

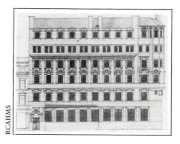

Employers' Liability Assurance Corp: Grecian iron framed in Nelson Mandela Place (demolished) by James Sellars, 1877.

St George's Church drawn by James Whitelaw.

offering a pattern of pilastered windows rising into a dormered Renaissance skyline. Not great architecture but contributing to the rich texture of the street. On the north side of St Vincent Place, the severe 1850-1 classical block running as far as Citizen Lane (**Nos 130-140**) is by James Robertson: the curtain-walled upper floors were added by J & J Laird, c.1960.

Clydesdale Bank, 150 Buchanan Street,
1981, G D Lodge & Partners
Contemporary banker's architecture: opulence and secrecy implied by dark reflective glass and bright chrome; a gesture to its setting in keeping the street frontage and the somewhat unsubtle billowing of windows. A crisp cornice rather than a recessive roofline would have made all the difference.

Western Club, 147 Buchanan Street,
1839-42, David & James Hamilton
A confident palazzo, advanced wings, majestic first floor windows, combining late Soane and mannerist motifs under a mighty cornice. Its strongly individual character may relate to a continental tour James Hamilton undertook in 1840. In its last years, the Club presented a picture of faded magnificence. Its interior was truly palatial with a vast imperial stair, huge public rooms, and bedrooms with Biedermeier sleigh beds of monumental proportions.

46**St George's Tron Church**, 1807, William Stark
A plain rectangle: pedimented back façade closing West George Street; and grandly Doric columns facing east down George Street. The tower has five stages, the topmost a Doric peristyle capped by a ribbed dome and an obelisk. Unexpectedly baroque for so deeply committed a neo-classicist, it is reminiscent of Hawksmoor in its severely detailed, concave elevations. In the galleried, flat-ceilinged interior, the most interesting features are the shallow vaults under the gallery, and the later marble pulpit.

47**Stock Exchange**, 1875, John Burnet (sen)
Superb early French Gothic, adapting a section of the Strand frontage of William Burges's London Law Courts submission of 1866. (It did not escape Burges's notice: he pasted Burnet's drawing of it, along with Lockwood's of his similarly derived Bradford Town Hall, into his personal copy of the Law Courts submission). Burnet caught his sense of scale very well, and the Mossman sculpture was worthy of the occasion. The figures at the capitals of the Buchanan Street entrance represent the four

Anne Dick

Mitchell Library

Above Stock Exchange as originally built. *Left* looking up Buchanan Street, from the Western Club, past the Stock Exchange, St George's Church to the Royal Scottish Academy of Music and Drama.

continents. J J Burnet extended the Exchange the whole length of the south side of St George's Place in 1904-6.

Nile, 77-81 Nelson Mandela Place,
1875, James Boucher
Richly sculptured, diapered and balconied four-storey block for stockbrokers Holms Kerr & Hedderwick; now a stylish bar. Identical façade on the other side at Nos 58-60 West Nile Street. **No 85**, currently a Pizza Hut returning round into West Nile Street, is skilful low-cost Italianate by Peddie & Kinnear, 1872, relying solely on fine proportions, the even rhythm of its arched windows and a bracketed cornice.

48 **Athenaeum**, 1886, J J Burnet
The principal floor is based upon the Arch of Constantine, astride a plain, channelled-stone plinth. Sculpture groups by Mossman who, as ever, rose to the occasion magnificently, and also provided the figures of Flaxman, Wren, Purcell and Reynolds in the attic. Of the equally Beaux-Arts interior, decorated in Burnet's favourite Japanese scheme of blue, yellow and gold, only a few fragments remain at the entrance.

RSAMD

Former Royal Scottish Academy of Music. The Athenaeum on its left; see also p. 149 and below.

Anne Dick

Royal Scottish Academy of Music,
1908-9, A N Paterson
Built as the Liberal Club to eclipse both the merchants' Western Club, and more particularly the Conservative Club on Bothwell Street, it was the result of a limited competition. Shallow-bayed, red sandstone elevations are punctuated by bold stacks. The impressive entrance rises to a vaulted stone and marble vestibule with a richly sculptured chimneypiece. Big-vaulted hall at first floor identified by huge windows and a balcony. No *grand escalier*; the emphasis had shifted to the elevator. The adjacent **Athenaeum Theatre**, 179 Buchanan Street, 1891-3, by J J Burnet presents a graceful, vertically proportioned, gabled front, with a canted bay cantilevered out from an arched recess—an American idea—topped by a niche. The stair tower, continuously mullioned to express the lift shaft, rises into a Tower of the Winds cupola.
Michaelangelesque (rather than Beaux Arts) statuary makes a first appearance. Simple, but effectively detailed, balconied auditorium, still with its original seats, which once followed the Japanese blue, yellow and gold colour scheme of the main building.

Tower Building, 1877, James Sellars
Circled corner rises into a pilastered drum (which
formerly had a truncated conical roof). Art
Movement details.

Britannia Building, 160-168 Buchanan Street,
1898, John A Campbell
Originally the British Workmen's and General
Assurance Association's Dundas House. A tall,
vigorously composed, narrow frontage elevator
building in which Campbell proved himself the equal
of Burnet (who had broken partnership with him in
the previous year). The arch and bay windows of the
Athenaeum are skilfully combined with a broad-
eaved, octagonal corner oriel window, ribbed
chimney stacks above.

George Hotel, 249 Buchanan Street,
1835-6, David and James Hamilton
The agreeable Edwardian bow front of the George
skilfully accommodates a westward shift in the axis of
the street; and incorporates the Cleland Testimonial
Building, designed by the Hamiltons for the
subscribers as a public tribute to the City's great
superintendent, James Cleland (see p. 71).

RIAS Library

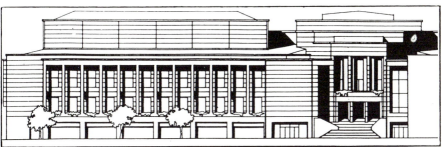

RMJM

WEST NILE STREET
Nos 82-86, 110, 114, 130-134 West Nile Street:
c.1808 are first generation survivors of West Nile
Street: plain classical buildings with architraved
windows, usually corniced at first floor, **No 134**
retains its rusticated ground floor.

Finlay House, 10-24 West Nile Street
1977, Scott Brownrigg & Turner
Decently stone-faced rectangular bays, opposite **No 7**,
1986-7, by Baxter Clark & Paul with the tinted
brown glass and red granite form beloved by
chartered surveyors at that date.

Top the Atheneum Theatre. *Above*
Glasgow Concert Hall-concept by Sir
Leslie Martin, designed by Robert
Matthew, Johnston Marshall &
Partners.

Royal London House, 54 West Nile Street, 1957-7, by Harold Branhill is a seven-storeyed building with a concrete frame rising out of the façade into the fashionable pergola at the recessed top floor. **106 West Nile Street** is small, but decent late classical, built by James Smith as the Victoria Baths in 1837. **Moncrieff House**, 1985-6, by Scott Brownrigg & Turner, is red granite with three oriels; and **Standard Life House** on the corner of West Regent Street, was designed by Cockburn Associates, mid 1970s. The only older building of real quality is **99-107 West Nile Street**, c.1858, by Alexander Thomson: a small three-storey office block, its top-floor window pilastrade reminiscent of the flank of his Caledonia Road Church.

Right Gordon Chambers. *Below* drawing of the *Glasgow Herald* Building by Charles Rennie Mackintosh.

[49]**Former Glasgow Herald Building, Mitchell Street**, 1893-5, Charles Rennie Mackintosh Surviving drawings leave no doubt that Mackintosh, still an assistant with Honeyman & Keppie, designed it. Much of the solidity of old Scots architecture: four storeys of deeply recessed, oblong openings emphasise the thickness of the walls. Sinuous, free-Renaissance dormer heads at the two floors over the main cornice. The slim octagonal corner tower flowers into a corbelled and galleried top (seemingly derived from the stair turret at James MacLaren's High School at Stirling), brilliantly conceived to close the long vista down West Nile Street. Effective use of small bits of high-quality sculpture.

The Library, The Royal Faculty of Procurators.

Anne Dick

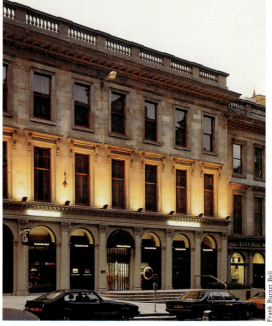

Above Mackintosh drawing for the Daily Record Building. *Top right* De Quincey's, Hope Street. *Right* centrepiece of Alexander Kirkland's design for the north side of Bothwell Street.

Hunterian Art Gallery, University of Glasgow

Anne Dick

Frank Burnet Bell

Above looking from the Blythswood Hill south down Wellington Street, the Royal Bank immediately on the left.
Above left interior of the Theatre Royal.
Left the view east down West George Street.

103

Above Blythswood Square looking east. *Right* sculptures from the Clyde Port Authority Building. *Below* figures from Charing Cross Mansions.

Gordon Chambers, 89-94 Mitchell Street,
1903-5, Burnet & Boston, & James Carruthers
Baroque red sandstone cliff at the opposite corner of
Mitchell Lane built for the publican David Ross who
had made a fortune in gold and cattle in Australasia.
It cost £32,500, an enormous sum at the time. The
elevation has giant two-storeyed openings over the
balustraded fifth-floor balcony. The **Gordon's** pub
front, with its etched and stained glass windows, and
the wrought iron fanlights and baroque lift shaft to
premises above, are all still intact.

Renfield Street looking north.

RENFIELD STREET
Part of the Blythswood feus promoted by William
Harley and his associates. Architecturally very rich
like Hope Street, the majority of its finest buildings
are side elevations of corner buildings fronting
Gordon Street, West George Street, St Vincent
Street, West Regent Street and Bath Street, under
which they are described. Linking these are one or
two buildings of interest.

Classic, 11-15 Renfield Street,
1914-16, James Miller
A tall, Beaux-Arts, white faience façade, very good of
its kind. Its Louis XVI cinema-restaurant interior by
John Ednie, was first modified and then burnt out.
Under reconstruction by G D Lodge, 1989.

Prudential Building.

Paramount Cinema, showing the impact of "night architecture".

RIAS Collection

50 **Odeon Film Centre**, 1934, Verity & Beverley
Built as the Paramount Cinema, once memorable for its fin-mullioned entrance corner, and its brilliant, neon 'night-architecture'. The superb Art Deco auditorium was tripled in 1969.

Pavilion Theatre, 1902-3, Bertie Crewe
Originally shiny buff terracotta (rendered matt by cleaning), a triple segmental pedimented façade to Renfield Street, and twin towers facing Renfrew Street. French interior.

Prudential, 28-36 Renfield Street,
1929, James Miller
American classic façade designed as a department store for James Woodhouse & Sons. Giant Ionic pilastered lower floors on the model of his Bank of Scotland on St Vincent Street: as there, Richard Gunn had a large hand in it.

Horse Shoe Bar, Drury Street, c. 1870
A singular composition of superimposed pilastrades with richly ornamented apron bands between them. The pub fascia, lit by elegant scrolled bracket lights, was lavishly remodelled between 1885 and 1887. It is still mercifully intact with its oval island bar, wall of mirrors and farrier statuette. Telegraphic stock market reports used to be received and posted for the convenience of those staying too long after lunch.

UNION STREET
Duncan's Hotel, Union Street, from 1802
Best of the plain, but distinctively proportioned, original four-storey tenements surviving on the west side.

Caledonian Chambers, 75-95 Union Street,
1901, Donald Mathieson & James Miller
Part of the reconstruction of Central Station treated as a separate building in the baroque idiom then current. Its seven-storey, 11 double-bay façade is divided horizontally by a cantilevered balcony, plain below but for a central pedimented and columned window, Ionic columned above, clasped between arched towers. Giant armorial, pedimented aedicules embracing two-storeyed bay windows, with sculpture by Albert Hodge.

Boots, corner Argyle Street, 1960, Colin Oakes
A blue and yellow Festival of Britain curving curtain-wall: most of it a veneer over the stone neo-Georgian façade of the Adelphi Hotel, by Bromley & Watkins. **28-40**, tall stone Art Deco built as the Georgic

restaurant by Whyte & Galloway, 1929,
commemorated the White Star Liner of that year.

50-76 Union Street, 1850s, William Lochhead
Important piece of early modern, cast-iron similar in
principle to the Spence warehouse in Jamaica Street.
The façade is divided by slim masonry strips into
eight oblong bays divided in turn by slim, Corinthian
cast-iron mullions.

51**Egyptian Halls, 84-100 Union Street**,
1871-3, Alexander Thomson
The building in which Thomson gathered all his
previous motifs into a single stupendous penultimate
composition. Cast-iron framed, its façade is
characteristic of Thomson's extraordinary originality
and intellect. The original shop fronts, deep
architraves with incised bands of anthemion
ornament, have been partly restored in recent years.
First and second floors are coupled-pilastered, but
within the first-floor columns is a secondary row of
pilasters with scrolled bracket capitals. The top floor
of squat columns, Indian in proportion but Egyptian
in detail, form a true eaves gallery.

Egyptian Halls.

RCAHMS

Top and above Atlantic Chambers.
Top right view up Hope Street at the St Vincent Street intersection with the Norwich Union Building on the left.

HOPE STREET
One of the five richest streets in Glasgow forming, together with Buchanan, Gordon, St Vincent and West George a notably concentrated block of architectural merit.

19-23 Hope Street, c.1875, possibly James Boucher
Festooned frieze at the second floor level, Ionic pilasters, conch tympana and a very bold attic composed of five pedimented windows clasped in six stacks.

52 **Atlantic Chambers, 43-47 Hope Street**, 1899, J J Burnet
A largely steel-framed office block, one of Burnet's finest designs, and the earliest to reflect American elevator buildings of the same vintage. Both elevations are distinctive: Hope Street is focused on a

Anne Dick

central chimney shaft, shooting up between oriel bays to bisect the deeply shadowed Doric eaves gallery; Cadogan Street has giant Doric pilasters emerging from between canted oriel bays—Chicago style, again with an eaves gallery.

Standard Life Building at the corner of Hope and Gordon Streets.

67 Hope Street.

67 Hope Street, 1899, Robert Thomson & Andrew Wilson
Stylishly detailed offices and printing works for the *Glasgow Evening News*. Bay windows in deeply shadowed arched recesses are united by a single curvaceous balcony. Excellent sculpture.

91-115 Hope Street, 1876-7, Peddie & Kinnear
The first really large commercial building (originally an hotel) in Glasgow—four and five storeys, with attics and garrets in its capacious French roofs. Yet the detail is pure Grecian, breaking into Corinthian columns at the twin pavilions of the Hope Street frontage.

106-108 Hope Street, 1894, Salmon & Gillespie
Tall, refined Flemish Renaissance gable with elongated Corinthian columns and superb sculpture (carved by W Ferris but clearly from models by a first-rate sculptor): probably designed by Gillespie.

RCAHMS

109

Lion Chambers.

53Daily Record, 20-28 Renfield Lane,
1900-1, Charles Rennie Mackintosh
A tall printing works of white brick, clasped by stone trim at top and bottom, composed skilfully to show to advantage in a narrow lane: boldly arched ground floor; fourth-floor oriel windows, to give movement over the pilastered intermediate floors; and dormer windows and angle turrets against the sky. The north elevation to St Vincent Lane displays the triangular tree motif which was to be the basis of so much of his detail at Derngate, Northampton, in 1915. Restored recently by the Miller Partnership. (Colour plate, p. 102)

54 157-167 Hope Street, 1902, John A Campbell
A Spanish Renaissance Alcazar in red sandstone. Campbell's supreme masterpiece, in which he showed himself fully the equal of his ex-partner J J Burnet. A tall, eight-storey cliff clasped between orielled, finialled angle towers, that facing West George Street Street with a circular turret. Save for the centre three projecting bays with balconies, aediculed with fine carving, all is plain until the seventh floor. Above that, a giant two-storey arcade rises from a balustraded balcony to a mighty cornice.

Beyond West George Street, Hope Street consists mainly of altered original houses on the corners of West Regent Street and Bath Street with approximately matching buildings erected on their back gardens.

55Lion Chambers, 172 Hope Street,
1904-7, James Salmon II & John Gaff Gillespie
White, gabled, eight-storey tower rising 90 ft from the pavement on a site only 33 by 46 ft. Reinforced concrete construction devised by the French engineers L G Mouchel and T J Gueritte of the Yorkshire Hennebique Company was adopted (the first Hennebique construction in Scotland). Square columns varying from 8 in to 13 in carry eight storeys of floor slabs and wall panels, 4.5 and 4 in thick respectively, to accommodate a basement printing works, a shop, law chambers and artists' studios at the very top. The wall panels were rendered in yellow stucco with a sparing use of modelled ornament, a *bas relief* armorial panel at first and second floors, and busts of judges at the angles of the oriel.

56Theatre Royal, Hope Street, 1867, George Bell; interior, 1895, C J Phipps
Built as James Baylis's Royal Colosseum, entered originally by an arcade from Cowcaddens. The clientele proved rough and in 1869 it became the replacement of the theatre in Dunlop Street. Bell

RCAHMS

inserted a pedimented front with arched windows, into a façade of some plain three-storey buildings. It masks a sumptuous interior. Phipps's magnificent auditorium, the equal of most built in London before 1900, is golden brown with three tiers of fiddle-shaped galleries facing a Corinthian-columned proscenium. It had been given up for dead when Scottish Opera made it its permanent home, commissioning a new foyer in the same idiom from Derek Sugden of Arup Associates, 1974-5. (Colour plate, p. 103)

McConnel's Building, 307-333 Hope Street, 1905-6, John Keppie
A long and unusually splendid City Improvement Trust tenement with a baroque grandeur more appropriate to the theatre opposite. Each unit has an armorial chimney breast flanked by sinuous, segmentally pedimented canted bays, clasped between five-storey oblong stair towers; domed at the Cowcaddens corner. The rear has railed galleries or platts leading to the flats while, in common with other model tenements of the period, the roof is a flat promenade with decorative iron railings at the concave parapets.

McConnel's Building.

GORDON STREET
Laid out by Alexander 'Picture' Gordon who bought the land opposite his fine new house to secure an open outlook from his windows. The south side corners to Buchanan and Mitchell Streets are the original classical, four-storey tenements of c.1815.

20-50 Gordon Street.

The rest, largely redeveloped between 1850 and 1890, forms one of the most architecturally distinguished streets in Glasgow.

19 Gordon Street, 1931, James Carruthers
A severe pilastered composition, modelled on Burnet & Tait's Kodak House in London. Superb Art Deco elevator doorpieces within.

Royal Bank, 1855-6, David Rhind
Rhind's finest surviving building: a majestic Italianate banking palazzo 11 bays long, divided 3-5-3 by broad pilasters of vermiculated rustication. The central bays rise a storey higher into a Corinthian colonnade of arched windows with a deep bracketed cornice. Superb detailing, head keystones, deeply recessed carved panels, and windows with segmental pediments at the centre of each division: all sculptured by Handyside Ritchie. Interiors replaced in 1937 by James McCallum with sculpture by J H Clark.

Woolwich Equitable, 18 Gordon Street,
1939-41, T Aikman Swan
Plain 1930s classic, with a black granite ground floor built originally for Scottish Amicable.

29-35 Gordon Street, c.1855 at the southern corner with Mitchell Street, is idiosyncratic late classical, with pilastered first-floor windows linked together.

57**Ca' d'Oro**, 1872, John Honeyman
An attempt to reproduce a contemporary version of Venice's celebrated Golden House with the new technology, developing John Baird and James Thomson's early experiments with cast-iron. Giant masonry arches sit upon Doric pilasters with vermiculated rustication, embracing the shops. Triple-arched cast-iron bays, with slim Corinthian shafts and circular attic windows enclose the three warehouse and workshop floors above. The whole is crowned with a concave, basket-weave, diapered cornice. Reconstructed back to its original appearance with additional bays on Union Street in 1988-9 by Scott Brownrigg & Turner.

20-40 Gordon Street, 1873, Peddie & Kinnear
A ruthlessly disciplined oblong block of business chambers, demonstrating mastery of the fashion for superimposed and interwoven ranks of pilasters. The frieze and the soffit members of the cornice combine into a deep enriched cavetto.

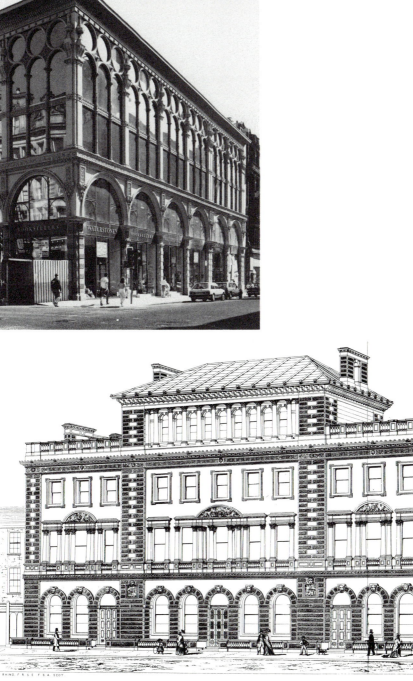

Left Ca' d'Oro. *Below* Royal Bank —
original perspective published in the
Building Chronicle.

Anne Dick

RIAS Library

42-50 Gordon Street, 1886, Clarke & Bell
Inventive, three-bay Renaissance building, built for
Royal Exchange Assurance. Boldly consoled and
pedimented entrance with a cameo of Hygeia at the
centre. The outer, twin shallow-canted bays are
clasped by pilasters bearing urns, an elaborately
dormered attic above. The adjacent **Saxone
Building, 52-58 Gordon Street**, had its corner cut
out and restyled by Westwood & Emberton for
Austin Reed, 1927.

65-69 Gordon Street, 1850, James Brown
One of the earliest of the really large blocks of
classical business chambers over shops, with a circled
corner with attic and corner dome. Badly in need of
restoration.

58 **Central Hotel**, 1879, Sir Rowand Anderson
Five-storey façade of a refined amalgam of early
Italian, Jacobean, and northern European elements—
notably at the tall, and admirably solid, pyramid-
roofed Germanic clock tower, the arched recess and
bay windows. In 1901-6, the station was doubled in
size on the western side and the hotel much extended
down Hope Street (Donald Mathieson as engineer
and James Miller as architect). Mathieson contributed
the roof of semi-elliptically arched girders, a great
deal more elegant than the original ones, and Miller
the huge, two-light early Italian train hall windows

Right Grosvenor Building with its
inappropriately added domed roofscape.
Below Central Hotel.

Anne Dick

Anne Dick

on Hope Street and the early Renaissance details of its extension over Argyle Street. The concourse is notable for the oval timber Torpedo Building. Formerly the waiting room and indicator screen where destination boards rattled the changes with unbelievable rapidity, it was converted to the Caledonian Centre in 1987, an elegant range of new shops being added in the same idiom.

The hotel interiors are still fairly complete: Anderson's fairly restrained early Renaissance, Miller's more demonstratively luxurious,—notably at the domed lounge area, with glass by Oscar Paterson and decorative detail and fittings by the Bromsgrove Guild, which projects out into the station's concourse.

60-70 Gordon Street, 1856-8,
Boucher & Cousland (altered)
The former R W Forsyth building began life as Black's warehouse, a three-storey palazzo of mildly Venetian character. In 1896 Forsyth commissioned J J Burnet to make it more fashionably stylish. The roof was raised a storey and mansarded, the corner taken out, a Corinthian dome with a caryatid attic inserted, and the interior replanned diagonally, leading to a magnificent quarter-circle stairwell on which the clientele could venerate the bronze bust of the founder by Sir W Reid Dick.

Grosvenor Building, 72-80 Gordon Street, 1859,
Alexander Thomson
A successful effort on the part of Alexander and his brother George Thomson to break into the premier warehouse league. George, a member of the congregation of the UP church which stood on the site, arranged to buy it to finance the building of the UP St Vincent Street Church (see p. 132). A and G Thomson's warehouse created a new architectural language: a giant pilastrade within a huge architraved frame, with a deeply recessed, consoled eaves gallery and incised ornament. The Ionic façade rising above into twin baroque domes was added by J H Craigie, of Clarke & Bell, 1902-7, to mark the building's conversion into the most sumptuous of Glasgow's restaurants with a German baroque banqueting hall at 2nd and 3rd floors (now gone).

Standard Life, 82-92 Gordon Street,
1890, James Thomson
Old-fashioned Italianate with canted bays at the ends, transformed by being heightened in the same way as Grosvenor, at the hands of his sons: superimposed Corinthian columns and French roofs.

Central station and Hotel was an heroic undertaking. The Glasgow & South Western Railway had refused the Caledonian running rights into its station at St Enoch's. So the Caledonian, and its ally the London North-Western, had no choice but to cross the river likewise, and bought its way from Bridge Street across the river, up Alston Street to Gordon Street. Central station was built in 1876-9 to designs by the Edinburgh engineers Blyth & Cunningham who adopted the graceless, transverse-pitched roofs, on the model of Edinburgh Waverley, carried on massive, trussed single-span girders. Sir Rowand Anderson was commissioned to wrap a magnificent headquarters office block round it, the necessary hotel accommodation being provided opposite at 91-115 Hope Street. The Caledonian thereafter changed its mind, and instructed Anderson to convert their offices into an hotel to outclass St Enoch's. The task took nearly three years, instead of the directors' sanguine estimate of one. Of Anderson's design *The Builder* commented in 1898: *One hesitates to classify its style....At the time it was built it might have been called 'Queen Anne' but it is more restrained than most of the architecture that was perpetrated in that Royal Lady's name.*

Part of the Caledonian Centre, Central station.

Anne Dick

Blythswood Square.

RCAHMS

BLYTHSWOOD NEW TOWN

Some time in the 1790s, *Mr Craig, architect in Edinburgh,* was engaged to produce a feuing plan which would relate sensibly to the street pattern already established in the first New Town around George Square. This may have been James Craig (1744-95), designer of Edinburgh's first New Town; for there proved to be more than a passing resemblance between what had been done in the capital and the layout now proposed for Blythswood. Here, too, was a grid set on a hill, the major streets in elongated east/west alignment, minor lanes and service mews in a parallel network. Yet there are major differences: the scale is smaller, the grid open-ended and, although there seems to have been a moment when West George Street might have emerged as the principal thoroughfare, there was no central axis in the plan comparable to Edinburgh's George Street. Nonetheless, the notion that Craig at the end of his life might have helped shape Glasgow's second New Town is intriguing. The street grid was set by Craig, supervised by estate surveyor William Kyle and modified (c.1819) by architect James Gillespie Graham. Conformity to the simple but elegant standards of late Georgian architecture was answered by legal titles, which required ashlar façades and slated roofs, forbade dormers and mansards, and specified a maximum three-storey-and-basement height. As a result, the street-to-street ranges running east/west and the aggregative terraces on the steeper inclines maintained a fine townscape of classical restraint.

By the 1820s, 'a distinctive Glasgow style had established itself' on Blythswood Hill: a plain, sauvely proportioned classical architecture of street-to-street terrace ranges. Houses, set back behind ironwork railings, were reached by short flights of

The Campbells of Blythswood

were one of Glasgow's oldest prominent mercantile families with a fine 17th-century mansion in the Briggait. In 1670, Provost Colin Campbell purchased the Blythswood Annexation Lands, a 470 acre estate centred upon Blythswood Hill. By the 1790s, Glasgow's expansion westwards was butting against the estate, which extended from present day West Nile Street west to Pitt Street, and from Argyle Street north to include Garnet Hill. The Campbells disentailed the estate, which had been in tailzie since 1739, and feued it off to enterprising speculators, who took the risk, and were sometimes bankrupted. So relentless was the City's move westward, that the estate proved a dripping roast for decades. Between 1799 and 1849, the Campbells rental income increased one hundredfold, with which they quit Glasgow and built the fine new classical mansion Blythswood at Renfrew (see *The South Clyde Estuary*) in 1820-2. 'Senex', writing in mid-century *Glasgow Herald* noted sarcastically how little of the wealth had benefited the city: 'We look in vain for the Campbells of Blythswood amongst the benefactors of the city.'

Blythswood Square in 1835.

Mitchell Library

steps spanning the basement areas below. Heights
were either two- or three-storey; end units—and
sometimes centres too—were emphasised by raised
elevation and subtle projection in plan. There were
tall first-floor windows, smart porches and banded
stonework along street-level storeys. It was a simple
formula, elegantly executed in crisp ochre ashlar
stonework, given added interest where housing
stepped down the steeper lower slopes of the hill.

Victorian and Edwardian commerce radically
altered the street scale of the lower slopes, though
some continuity of plot-width façade was maintained.
Tall infill buildings appeared, while extra storeys
were added irregularly to the original ranges.
Twentieth-century redevelopment has proved still less
circumspect: whole street blocks intrude their ill-
conceived bland bulk into the calculated domestic
restraint of the Blythswood Hill townscape.

59 **Blythswood Square**, c.1823-9, John Brash
Originally Garden Square, after its developer
Hamilton William Garden who became insolvent and
had to flee to USA, the Square consists of four
identical, late classical terraces of fine ashlar, facing
the central garden. The only modelling, save on the
eastern side where James Miller created a central
entrance to the Royal Scottish Automobile Club in
1923, is created by five-bay end pavilions,
accentuated by Ionic porches. The entire east terrace
interior is stylishly French inside, as remodelled by
Miller for the RSAC. Note the 1908 door inset by
Charles Rennie Mackintosh at **No 5** for the Lady

*'**The patrician locality** of the
Blythswood grounds, where are
situated Blythswood Square,
Elmbank Crescent, Woodside
Crescent etc, are built and laid out
with a degree of magnificence worthy
of Merchant Princes of the West.
This is called the new part of town;
and with the exception of Moray
Place in Edinburgh and some of the
squares in London, the crescents and
square we have named are unequalled
in architectural beauty and unity by
the buildings in any part of the
Kingdom. The houses are built of
durable white freestone and so
substantially constructed without that
they are destined to endure for ages.
Here is congregated all that is most
refined, elevated and opulent in a
mercantile and manufacturing
aristocracy.'*

St Jude's Church.

D Walker

No 7 Blythswood Square has pride of place in what Jack House has dubbed Glasgow's *Square Mile of Murder* (1961). From 1856 this was the home of the architect James Smith (1808-63), designer of the McLellan Galleries on Sauchiehall Street (1855) and father of Madeleine Smith, who was to become perhaps the most notorious young woman in mid-Victorian Glasgow.

The Smiths occupied only the ground floor and basement of an imposing end terrace block—a tight squeeze for a family of seven with three servants, but a most respectable address nonetheless. Madeleine and her younger sister Janet shared a basement bedroom with pavement level windows round the corner in Blythswood Street, a fact to prove fatally convenient for Madeleine's lover Pierre Emile L'Angelier. Madeleine and L'Angelier had established their liaison in 1855 exchanging what to Victorian sensibilities was a torrid series of love letters and meeting secretly in Glasgow and at the Smiths' seaside home in Rhu. By 1857 Madeleine had begun to blow hot and cold, and when the rich and respectable Billy Minnoch—soon to be her fiancé—moved into the flat above the Smiths, L'Angelier's fate was sealed. In the early morning of 22 March L'Angelier died in agony, poisoned by arsenic. The charge of murder laid against Madeleine was Not Proven, a verdict at which the whole court *erupted into wild applause*. Madeleine subsequently married George Wardle, a drawing teacher in Plymouth, through whom she entered the circle of William Morris to become a 'renowned Bloomsbury hostess'. She died peacefully in New York in 1928 aged 92.

Artists' Club, and the powerfully curved rear elevation of **No 26** at 177 West Regent Street—the only house to retain a high-quality original interior.

St Jude's Church, 1838-9, John Stephen Stephen's addiction to the Greek Revival was masterly and creative as he showed in his warehouses in James Watt Street (see p. 50) and, best of all, in his Testimonial School in Renfrew built to honour one of the Blythswood Campbells. Here, a huge battered door of Grecian extraction is creatively elaborated, with a skill which anticipates Alexander Thomson. Until the 1960s, it was crowned with a miniature version of the Lysicrates Monument, an element also favoured by Stephen in his Blythswood Testimonial School tower (see *The South Clyde Estuary* in this series).

BATH STREET

Opened in 1800 by James Cleland, the City
Superintendent, and named after William Harley's
Baths. The east end of the street is still largely
composed of the original two- to four-storey Georgian
houses, now much modified.

38 Bath Street, 1861, James Salmon
Built as the Mechanics' Institution, with a giant
order of unfluted Greek Ionic columns, the baroque
upper floors were added by Arthur Hamilton when it
was converted to offices.

Transport Department, 46 Bath Street,
c.1850, John Baird II
A four-storey office building with façades of severest
superimposed pilastrades, the windows being grouped
in triplets. The baroque doorpiece and top storey
were added in 1904 by the city engineer A B
MacDonald. The south side of Bath Street begins
with plain three- and four-storey Georgian tenements,
interrupted by the towering six-storey red sandstone
pile of **11-15**, 1901, one of the few genuinely bad
Edwardian buildings in the city.

Lower Georgian proportions return at **Nos 115** and
121 Wellington Buildings turning the corner to
Wellington Street with a balustraded French
roofscape, and **No 129**, 1910-11, by H E Clifford,
grandly columned and corniced, intrude on this
reversion with greater dignity than most of their
modern neighbours. The 1840 terraces at **Nos
143-173** and **152-178** preserve a largely intact
streetscape thanks to some good restoration. Around
the corner in West Campbell Street, the Post-Modern
1986 extension by Boys Jarvis is perhaps a little too
provocatively self-conscious, but demonstrates effort
to match the dignity of the old.

William Harley

None of Glasgow's benefactors
seems more intensely to have
personified that typically Scottish
combination of compassionate
moral rectitude and shrewd
business sense. Arriving in
Glasgow in 1789 aged 19, Harley
found work in the cotton trade,
and a year later, set up business at
the corner of George Square.
Within three years, he had become
a prosperous manufacturer of
turkey-red checked gingham.
Harley did much to alleviate the
deplorable conditions of the city's
poor, set up highly successful
Sabbath schools and formulated a
series of proposals for the
organisation of compulsory
education. In 1802 he bought large
stretches of the Blythswood Estate
lands at Sauchy Haugh. Here he
built his house, Willowbank, and
established tea gardens to which
Glaswegians flocked for a country
jaunt. For a time Blythswood Hill
was even known as Harley's Hill.
Soon he was sinking wells and
piping fresh water to a large
reservoir tank constructed in 1804
from which his water carts
supplied the city's needs. He
erected fine baths (hence Bath
Street) and in 1810 built an
immense dairy in the same
neighbourhood. Realising the
potential of the second New Town,
he began to undertake speculative
building developments but, caught
by the economic crisis of 1815-16
he suddenly *went under forever* in
financial ruin. An invitation from
the Empress of Russia to establish
another large dairy might have
restored his fortunes. *En route* for
St Petersburg he died suddenly.

RCAHMS

Bath Street looking east.

Above West Campbell Street office block by Boys Jarvis. *Below* Bath Street looking west.

Anne Dick

C McKean

Glasgow Art Club, 185 Bath Street,
1834, John Brash (?)
No 185 Bath Street had been a doctor's residence, one of several which turned this crest-of-the-hill range, orginally known as Athol Place, into the Harley Street of the Blythswood New Town. John Keppie's alterations to the Art Club, 1892, an enriched decor for the entrance hall, created a pillared dining hall on the ground floor and added a large roof-lit gallery or 'smoking room' where the back gardens had been. The oak woodwork of the gallery, notably the tall chimney pieces of two end fireplaces, are 'in Italian Renaissance style, freely treated', according to a note on a sketch by Keppie's young assistant, Charles Rennie Mackintosh. Free indeed, for what emerges is nothing less than Glasgow Style.

181-199 Bath Street and **182-200 Athol Place**,
1833, John Baird I
Ionic porches on both sides of the street, that at **194** with coupled columns and flanked by two wide segmental windows successfully cut from the original façade (now plasticised).

60 **202-218 Adelaide Place**, begun 1839, Robert Black
An entire palace-fronted block stepping down the hill, pilastered, porched and pedimented; the grandest achievement of the entire estate. Only part of the balancing range across the street, from **201** to **205**, now survives. The remainder of the block is taken up by the raised temple of the grandiloquent but underscaled **Adelaide Place Baptist Church**, 1875, by T L Watson.

Elgin Place Congregational Church,
1865, J Burnet
Magnificent raised Roman temple. The detail of the great Ionic portico which rises from Pitt Street and the five tall consoled windows along Bath Street is impeccable. No longer a church, but a night club, its pagan formula adapts well to the city's booming night life.

61 **St Stephen's Renfield Church**,
1849-52, J T Emmett
Bulbous tenements at **Nos 244-256** lead on to Bath Street's only surviving steeple—and a good one, too, although badly scraped. It seems ill served now by Munro & Partners' later halls and offices surrounding an incongruous open forecourt, although the effort to maintain the scale was welcomed at the time.

RCAHMS

RCAHMS

Hunterian Museum

62 **King's Theatre**, 1904, Frank Matcham
Uneasily composed mannerist froth in red sandstone.
Interior not quite so impressive as the late lamented
Empire but still Matcham at his very best: scroll
pedimented proscenium, Corinthian arcaded flanks
with conch semi-domes and serpentine balustrades.

Opposite is a slow tenemental curve to the street
wall from **268** to **276**, 1850-3. The other attraction
hereabouts is at **266**, the 1903 **Griffin** bar (formerly
the King's Arms), designed by William Reid in
Glasgow Style woodwork and glass. Beyond the
King's Theatre is **Mitchell House**, 1985, an
abstemious Chicago-style office block by Thorburn
Twigg Brown & Partners, in immaculate red brick.

Top Elgin Place Congregational (now
Follies). *Left* Griffin (formerly King's
Arms). *Above* Muirhead Bone's drawing
of Adelaide Place and St Stephen's
Renfield Church.

Above 4 West Regent Street. *Below* Prudential Building.

WEST REGENT STREET

Originally part of William Harley's Blythswood feus, although little original survives downhill.

4 West Regent Street, 1858-60, J A Bell
Very grand business chambers for Archibald Orr Ewing, in full Billings' baronial fig with oriels, deep machicolated parapets and elaborate crowstepped gables. Its eastern end being demolished for Standard Life House in 1974, what survives is still impressive enough to justify restoration.

63 **Prudential Building, 48-50 West Regent Street**, 1890, Alfred Waterhouse
Brick baronial blended into Waterhouse's characteristic Flemish form, with generous stone dressings. Superb Moorish tiled business hall now has an exotic atmosphere as **De Quincey's Restaurant**. (Colour plate, p. 102)

Castle Chambers, 51-57 West Regent Street, 1898-1902, James Carruthers
One of the most sumptuous *fin-de-siècle* blocks in the city, built for the MacLachlan brothers, brewers, distillers, restaurateurs and stud-owners. It contained their Palace Restaurant, office headquarters, and extensive chambers for rental in red sandstone baroque, towering eight storeys on Renfield Street with an octagonal corner. The august girls tucked between its consoled cantilever brackets are by Ernest Gillick.

56-58 West Regent Street, 1986, Comprehensive Design
Six-storey, Post-Modern, narrow-frontaged office block, its façade a clever variation upon the Edwardian canted-bay window motif. Note the blue railings and broken pediment. Opposite **61-69 West Regent Street**, 1988 by Scott Brownrigg & Turner, is an ambitious block in contemporary Glasgow style, with red sandstone oriels.

81 to 107 West Regent Street, 1830s
Two-storey-and-basement terrace stepping irregularly down the hill; **95** has a neatly added second floor; **100**, 1900-4, a former Masonic Hall, by J L Cowan, presents an intruding, red sandstone façade, niched, gabled and bayed, rising into a new two-storeyed mansard. **105-107** were remodelled internally by Alexander Thomson, c.1872. The later numbers **113-143**, c.1850, and **130-154a**, both 1850, are still less uniform: many with an extra storey added and several now no more than façade shells. **No 113** is notable for its central porch which has half-fluted

C McKean

RCAHMS

Left West Regent Street and the Deaf Institute. *Below* Beaten Glasgow Style panel at 79 West Regent Street by James Salmon, 1903.

columns and swagged capitals; **Nos 125-139** were rebuilt in a more unified form by G D Lodge, 1986.

Institute for the Adult Deaf & Dumb, 158 West Regent Street, 1893-4
A particularly clever design by Robert Duncan in which the corner offices and the **Ross Memorial Church**, 1931, by Norman Dick, are blended back into the prevailing three-storey streetscape.

WEST GEORGE STREET
Originally Camperdown Place, named after the great naval victory to correspond with St Vincent Place to the south, it consisted of terrace houses built in the early 1800s, although nothing of that date survives downhill. The earliest is the 1810 **No 110**, uphill, which survives with its Ionic porch.

Bank of England, 21 West George Street, 1981, Walter Underwood & Partners
Fortress-like as befitting a cash distribution centre: its solid brown marble façade with its semicircular eaves rhythm conveys a solidity in contrast with the prevailing reflective-glass money boxes. **Consort House**, 1974, opposite, by Miller & Black, replaced James Gillespie Graham's elegant Roman Doric George Street Independent Church of 1819.

Connal's Building, 34 West George Street, 1899, J B & W A Thomson
A tower-like six-storey and attic building modelled on the Ritter Inn, Heidelberg, its details therefore 16th century. Onion corner dome, all with sculptured locomotives, ships and portrait heads of the great engineers and ironmasters, James Watt, J B Neilson, William Dixon and Connal himself among others, sculpted by James Young.

West George Street: Connall's Building on the right.

Anne Dick

WEST GEORGE STREET

West George Street looking west: note the typically Glaswegian square around the Church. *Below* Royal Faculty of Procurators.

John McKean

Anne Dick

36 West George Street, 1871, James Thomson
This building for John Orr Ewing illustrates how
Thomson's style had changed over the previous
twenty-eight years: severe with banded rustication at
the square-columned porches.

64 **Royal Faculty of Procurators,
62 West George Street**, 1854, Charles Wilson
The finest surviving Glasgow example of the
Venetian Renaissance craze which swept the western
world from Warsaw to Portland, Oregon, in the mid
1850s. Finely sculptured frieze and concave panelled
ingoes, as well as Law Lord portrait keystones by
Handyside Ritchie. A gilded stair, with richly groin-
vaulted aisles, divided by square Corinthian columns,
leads to the outstanding bust-lined Library; in its
own scale and period, as fine an interior as
Edinburgh's Signet Library. (Colour plate, p. 101)

91-93 West George Street,
1911-13, Burnet & Boston
A masterly red-sandstone office block on a restricted
site, its seven storeys emphasised by the unbroken
verticals of its oriels and chimney shafts. Designed
just as American and London classic fashions were
taking over, it proves the native neo-baroque idiom
had lost none of its force.

101 West George Street, 1892-5, William Leiper
No expense was spared for the Sun Fire & Life
Assurance Company, and the French were
sufficiently impressed to award it a silver medal at
the Paris Exhibition of 1900. Its domed octagonal
corner, corbelled out to a greater girth, set the
Glasgow fashion for such. Much superb sculpture by
Birnie Rhind, not only at the deep friezes and at the
pediment on Renfield Street, but within the business
hall, whose chimneypiece has an armorial overmantel
panel of the sun supported by angels in coloured
marble.

65 **Royal Bank, 92-98 West George Street,**
1930, James Miller
Superb, attenuated bank, tall, slender and
authoritative. Miller's predilection for white
architecture expressed in Portland stone with
simplified, fluted pilasters, Art Deco capitals, and flat
and stylised cornice. **Nos 100-110** West George
Street, 1988, by Baron Bercott, is bay-windowed
Post-Modern, with an arcaded top.

Royal Bank.

RIAS Library

Right Scottish Widows before alteration.
Above 100-110 West George Street.

James Sellars House.

Scottish Widows, 112-114 West George Street,
1868, David Bryce
One of Bryce's finest palazzi, five bays wide to St
Vincent Street and nine to Renfield Street, originally
with an arched ground floor, and first-floor pilastered
and pedimented windows. Shops have been inserted
on the Renfield Street frontage, and in 1958 Walter
Underwood added a floor, removed the balconies and
blanked off the heads of the ground-floor windows.

Pearl Assurance Co, 133-137 West George Street,
1897, James Thomson
The first of the giant six-storey office blocks built at
the turn of the century, which reflected the arrival of
electric elevators and improved equipment at the Fire
Department. Caught between old-fashioned Italianate
and free German Renaissance and somewhat
improbably described as Venetian at the time.
Heavily consoled second-floor windows and
superimposed columns on the long Hope Street
frontage, with an arcaded eaves gallery of polished
granite shafts above.

Clydesdale Bank, 134-136 West George Street,
1867, John Burnet
A simple well-proportioned palazzo. The
neighbouring **Provincial Insurance Building,
138-140 West George Street**, 1859-60, by James
Thomson was built as three-storey with a finely
detailed arched and rusticated ground floor, later
heightened, c.1900, and given a double porch with a
curious order. Note the even more curious solecism
of a quatrefoiled Gothic balustrade in a Renaissance-
style building.

James Sellars House, 144-146 West George Street,
1877-80, James Sellars
Predominantly French, it marks the architect's rapid
shift from the influence of Thomsonesque Greek, the
pilastraded top floor being the only remaining trace.
Built as the New Club, its giant pedimented doorway
dominates a ground floor of large portholes, with a
row of five deep windows above, whose windows are
set in a low-relief frieze. The sculpture, of
uncommonly high quality throughout, is by William
Mossman. **Ocean Chambers**, 188-192 West George
Street, 1900, by R A Bryden, has six red sandstone
storeys of ebullient eclecticism catholic enough to
mix almost everything from Gothic to baroque.

Bank of Scotland, 163-167 West George Street,
1859-60, James Thomson
Italianate, setting the standard for Thomson business
blocks for the next ten years. The cruelly disfiguring
doorpiece is typical of bankers' 1950s taste.

66**196 West George Street**, c.1830
The finest surviving house in the Blythswood New
Town. Its five-bay front is given tasteful symmetrical
emphasis by steps, porch, pediment and scrolled
chimney stack. **Gate House** at **201**, originally the
Burns-Aitken Building, by John McLeod, 1881, may
be second generation but its richly eclectic façades
fully merit the conservation they have received from
G D Lodge.

196 West George Street.

St Vincent Street: *Top right* — in 1834. *Right* — as it is today. *Top* looking east, the Scottish Amicable followed by the Hatrack on the left. *Above* interior of 218.

ST VINCENT STREET

Opened in 1804 and named after the sea battle of St Vincent, St Vincent Street consisted of very grand terraced houses stepping up the flank of Blythswood Hill, mostly developed after 1820. By the 1850s, those closest to the city centre were already being replaced by business chambers, and redevelopment has continued ever since. The best survivors of first generation houses are to be found at the highest point of **Blythswood Hill**. The terrace at **Nos 206-228** retains an intact palace-front, 1825-30, with an off-centre Ionic porch; altered windows above belong to J J Burnet's 1899 remodelling. Burnet also provided some spectacular Beaux-Arts interiors at 67 **232-242** for the Royal College of Physicians and Surgeons. The five-bay **242** is especially good. The west end of the range was replaced in 1875 by the giant Windsor House at **250**, originally an hotel, by James Thomson. **Nos 185-213**, c.1825, also incomplete, have been indiscriminately increased in height. **219-245**, c.1825 are better, but sadly compromised by the second floor of 221. Downhill, the commercial push has effected a total transformation: close-packed cliffs full of Victorian and Edwardian quality.

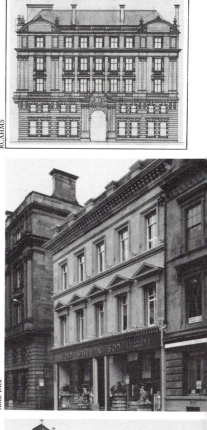

Co-operative Bank, 47 St Vincent Street, 1899, J M Peddie and G Washington Browne
Giant neo-baroque palace block (result of a competition for which Mackintosh produced a superb baroque design, see p. 95) sure in proportion and inventive in detail. Its great doorpiece and rippling curvilinear balconies are more central European than English. Impressive domed banking hall within, coupled black marble columns with swagged Ionic capitals and a baroque door.

John Smith & Sons, 49-61 St Vincent Street, c.1850, J T Rochead
A splendid Renaissance palazzo whose ground floor has long gone. The Tuscan aedicules and great cornice, restored in 1987, testify to the quality of the original design and show great skill in giving impact to a relatively short frontage. The bookshop has formed part of Glasgow publishing and bookselling life for nigh on two centuries.

67-69 St Vincent Street, c.1872, J J Stevenson
Queen Anne block, segmental pediments with cartouche bulls' eyes and columns over shallow, canted bays; and cleverly picking up themes from the splendid palazzo block at **81-91,** possibly by David Rhind. It has Rhind's windows, sculptured architraves, twin arch-linked chimneys and bold cornice; and unusually—the original shops, recently restored. Note **Caskie & Co's, 79,** with its spacious interior of slim Corinthian columns, by Cooper Cromar.

Bank of Credit and Commerce International, 78 St Vincent Street, 1912-13, A D Hislop
Pioneer Glasgow example of the new American classical style: giant ground floor Doric columns (a very American eagle-like Phoenix at the angle) and severe upper floors with subtle gradations of emphasis in the window architraves. Fine entrance hall with a groin vault on Doric columns. The carving and bronze work was executed by the Bromsgrove Guild. It marked the end of the native Glasgow baroque.

84-94 St Vincent Street, 1909, John A Campbell & A D Hislop
The first building in Glasgow to be fully steel-framed (ie with a front wall which was not load-bearing); and the first to be built in Portland stone. It marks

Top National Bank of Scotland (now Co-operative Bank). *Middle* John Smith & Sons. *Above* Nos 81-91 St Vincent Street.

129

84-94 St Vincent Street.

In how many Scottish towns did George Street become one of the 18th century's longest and straightest streets? Edinburgh, Aberdeen, Paisley... and, for a time, it seemed it would be the same in Glasgow. Not only did George Street stretch back into the Old Town as far east as High Street but it climbed relentlessly westward, dignified by the building of William Stark's steeple at St George's Church (*qv*), deliberately moved there by the Council in 1807 in preference to their earlier choice on the line of St Vincent Street. But West George Street, exhausted by its climb up Blythswood Hill, is brought to a halt by Holland Street. Instead, it is **St Vincent Street**, which links the Merchant City westwards, to become the central artery of the Blythswood New Town.

the beginning of the 1920s and 30s predilection for white architecture. Oriel bays, soaring through the deeply shadowed bracket cornice, are built out from the main façade in stepped planes, presumably the result of Campbell & Hislop's association with the German-American architect Pullich. The rear elevation of steel casement bays by Henry Hope overlooking St Mary's Court is again white, but in brick. The simple classical frontage discreetly linking them at **80-82** is by Laird & Napier, 1938.

TSB, 93 St Vincent Street, 1924, Andrew Balfour
Somewhat uncertain American classic with huge baroque armorial doorpiece, and windows in a rhythm of pairs and triples.

96-101 St Vincent Street, 1853, Clarke & Bell
Remnant of a palazzo for the North British Assurance Company, now without its arcaded, Ionic-columned ground floor. The Corinthian-columned first floor, and the spiralled architraves of the second, remain to give a hint of the quality of what has been lost and could still be recovered.

Carswell's, 101-3 St Vincent Street, 1876, James Thomson
Corinthian-pilastered China Merchant's palace with a channelled ground floor raised up on a podium of shops.

Scottish Mutual Assurance, 105-113 St Vincent Street, 1912, Frank Southorn
Somewhat unusual: Ionic-pilastered bays jettied out on massive second floor balconies, with seated figure sculpture.

115-117 St Vincent Street, 1865, John Burnet
Like so many bank and insurance buildings of this vintage, there are twin porches, one for the original (Union) Bank, one for the business chambers above. The first floor is grand: windows set in a colonnade of coupled Ionic columns which break forward into pediments at centre and ends.

68 **Bank of Scotland, 110-120 St Vincent Street**, 1924, James Miller
The Bank's primary west of Scotland presence: immensely imposing, since it was the HQ of the Union Bank and sought to eclipse the Edinburgh head office. A design derived from York and Sawyer's Guaranty Trust, 140 Broadway, New York, illustrated in the *Architectural Review, USA*, in 1913 (a copy of which had been lent by Alfred Lochhead

HEAD OFFICE OF THE UNION BANK OF SCOTLAND LIMITED, ST VINCENT STREET, GLASGOW

to Miller's chief draughtsman, Richard Gunn). Giant Ionic columns embraces the first three floors. The Doric-columned banking hall has just been restored.

Above Bank of Scotland — presentation drawing by James Miller.
Below 142 St Vincent Street and its neighbour the Hatrack.

130-136 St Vincent Street, 1876, James Thomson
The junction of St Vincent Street with Hope Street is the most architecturally spectacular in Glasgow. Nos **130-36** (a second palace for the same china merchant of **101-103**), is late-classical with refined Corinthian detail. The other three corners are examples of *fin-de-siècle* taste. First, **Liverpool, London and Globe**, 119-123 St Vincent Street, 1898, by James Thomson (although his sons John and William were probably the designers): a huge red sandstone pile of north European early Renaissance inspiration providing wonderful townscape. Onion-domed octagonal oriel at the corner, all decked out with some extremely good sculpture. The west corner, the former **Norwich Building**, 125-7 St Vincent Street, 1898, by John Hutchison, is another northern European mannerist pile in red sandstone, its canted corner rising into a circular conical roofed tower, with bull's eye windows. **142** St Vincent Street, 1899, by Frank Burnet & Boston, is remarkable for what could be extracted from a redeveloped Georgian house plot. Pedimented Ionic entrances on the narrow St Vincent Street frontage, slim corbelled octagonal corner rising into a broad eaved top (inspired by Mackintosh's in Mitchell Street), and the long elevation to Hope Street with recessed canted bays under a deep cornice, and a richly sculptured arcaded attic.

John McKean

Above The Hatrack. *Below* 200 St Vincent Street.

RCAHMS

142a-144 St Vincent Street,
1899-1902, James Salmon II
One of the Glasgow Style's greatest achievements:
ten floors of rippling red sandstone and glass within
a single terrace house plot. The façade is full of flat-
capped cornicing, mouldings and sculpture (probably
by Derwent Wood) which melt back into the stone.
Wrought iron and stained glass add to the building's
liveliness. Its now-missing peaked roofscape earned it
the nickname 'Hatrack'.

Scottish Amicable Building,
150 St Vincent Street, 1972-5, King Main & Ellison
Although occupying several original plots, it responds
well to the stepped nature of the original streetscape
by the rhythm of its tinted glass square-cut bay
windows. **No 153** St Vincent Street, 1904, Leiper &
McNab, is a tall red sandstone slab with distinctive
Renaissance detail, squashed beneath the top floor of
its James Miller neighbour, which was later
cantilevered over it: an index to the demand for
modern floor space at the time.

69 **200 St Vincent Street**, 1925-7, J J Burnet
Confidently corniced like a Florentine palazzo but
just as proud of its smooth cubic modernism, this
majestic building is a Scottish response to Burnet's
Adelaide House in London: windows punched
through stone walls, and soaring chimney stacks.
Plain elegance, save at ground level, where a
beautifully modelled arcade has been judiciously
enriched by figures over the columns at the entrance.
Burnet's last major work in Scotland.

West over the hill, the balance of the street, at first
high then lower, is disrupted. While early c. 1840
terraced houses at **260-284** St Vincent Street step
down the northern side, the immense glazed bulk of
Hugh Martin & Partners' **Britoil Building**, 1983-8,
looms across the street: a colossus of tinted glass and
purply granite more appropriate in scale and style to
those motorway margins of the inner city than to the
historic character and scale further east.

70 **St Vincent Street Church**,
1858-9, Alexander Thomson
Seen all the way from George Square, the powerful
tower engrosses Egyptian, Graeco-Roman, perhaps
even Indian motifs in uniquely inventive
combination. Alongside, a temple to Calvinist
worship seems to straddle its massive plinths of halls
and offices which are built out from the street slope
south with fortress-like solidity. Yet the floor of the
kirk is sunk within the plinth itself. Thomson had
Solomon's Temple actively in mind when designing.

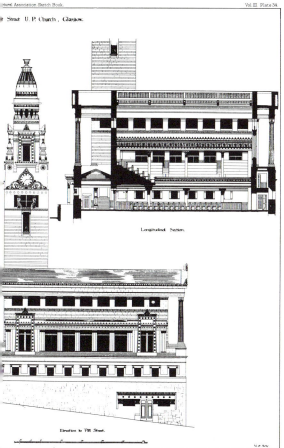

Stroot . U. P. Church . Glasgow.

Longitudinal Section.

Elevation to Pitt Street.

ry

RCAHMS

Above and left St Vincent Street Church by Alexander Thomson. *Below* Coats Viyella by SBT Architects, 1984. *Bottom* Britoil.

SBT

Hugh Martin

Darkly implacable to the street, the church conceals a lofty galleried interior sumptuous with light and colour. Vivid and rich red, blues and greens enrich columns, capitals, cornices and friezes, in almost medieval contrast to the austere anthemion leaves, and magisterial clarity of the stonework outside.

St Columba Church, 1902-4, Tennant & Burke A Gothic spire, 200 ft high, also seen over the hill from the city centre. Good carving, compromised perhaps by too much rough-faced stone. Early French style within.

Royal Bank, Bothwell Street.

4-26 Bothwell Street (Colour plate, p. 102)
1849, Alexander Kirkland & John Bryce
A long, now-incomplete range of shops and offices.
Central and east-end emphasis intact, the terrace has
a balustraded parapet, and an almost Venetian arcade
at street level. Recently restored and converted partly
by T M Miller & Partners and partly by Frank
Burnet Bell & Partners. The cubic, white, rather
Mayan classicism of the **Royal Bank** (formerly
Commercial), 1934, by James Miller, has replaced
the west pavilion of Kirkland's design. Note the
curtain-wall metal spandrels behind the giant
columns. In thrifty fashion, the upper storeys were
built as lettable offices. Didactic bas-reliefs by Gilbert
Bayes. It contrasts dramatically with the next street
block of office buildings, originally the Central
Thread Agency, five storeys almost salaciously
drenched in mannerist detail by David Barclay,
1891-1901.

15-20 Bothwell Street, 1890, Robert Ewan
Big red stone shipping offices with typical
Renaissance detail and modelling.

Mercantile Chambers, 1897-8, James Salmon II
An entirely unorthodox composition full of
fascinating Glasgow Style details and sculpture by
Derwent Wood. Real progress at the rear, in
Bothwell Lane, in the curtain-wall of shallow canted
bays. The formula was used by James Salmon in
Lion Chambers (see p. 110), partially taken up by
Mackintosh in his *Daily Record* building (see p. 110)
and most spectacularly exploited in the white brick
cliff which John A Campbell raised above St Mary's
Lane (see p. 130).

71 **Scottish Legal Life**, 1927, Wylie Wright & Wylie
Particularly majestic, American-inspired classical
street-block, chosen by competition. In contrast to
the solid frame of eaves, cornice, and banded quoins
and base, the new curtain-wall architecture of the
1920s can be seen emerging between the columns in
the building's three street façades: simultaneously
powerful and subtle design.

100 Bothwell Street, 1987, Holmes Partnership
Most of the rest of Bothwell Street is now given over
to the kind of office block architecture that could be
anywhere and should be nowhere. This building is
more sophisticated than most of the glass-wrapped
blocks hereabouts. American in influence, it is
dominated by a tall entrance tower and recesses the
ground floor to create space at street level. Its bland
sheen is poor exchange, however, for the baronial

BLYTHSWOOD HOLM
Construction on the southern
slopes of Blythswood Hill was
delayed by indecision over the
street layout. Although plots along
Argyle Street sold speedily, it took
several decades for the area
between Cadogan Street and St
Vincent Street to be built up. One
plan proposed to continue Gordon
Street westwards, as Melville
Street. Another envisaged a new
square at the west end of Gordon
Street to be '*another distinguishing
feature in our city architecture*'.
Gillespie Graham's plan of 1820
reasserted the grid-iron, delineating
Waterloo Street for the first time,
but showing Blythswood Terrace
and Gordon Street running parallel
to the north. It was not until mid-
century that **Bothwell Street**
came into existence through the
efforts of the entrepreneur James
Scott and his architect Alexander
Kirkland, whom Scott took to
Paris.

Below and right Mercantile Chambers with its statue in barley-sugar columns. *Bottom* Scottish Legal Life.

C McKean

Above Waterloo Chambers. *Above right* Bothwell Street. *Below* Heron House. *Bottom* Post office.

PIAS Library

Romanesque exuberance of the former **Christian Institute & YMCA**, 1878-80 and 1895-6, designed by John McLeod, later enlarged by Clarke & Bell and R A Bryden to occupy the entire street block.

Heron House, 1969, Derek Stephenson & Partners Carefully proportioned, sited and stepped to acknowledge and frame Thomson's St Vincent Street Church. Yet still too immense. At the end of the street, the Venetian arcades of **Eagle Buildings**, 1854, by Alexander Kirkland, though cocooned in scaffolding, are an embarrassing reproach to so much mediocrity.

Waterloo Chambers, 15-23 Waterloo Street, 1899, J J Burnet
The first of Burnet's American-scaled elevator office blocks, intended originally to have two more storeys which proved to be beyond the firemaster's reach. It is a vertical stack of boldly advanced and deeply recessed Greek and Renaissance details, balconied and balustraded with impunity. Giant Ionic order for connoisseurs of Beaux-Arts design. W T Oldrieve & Sir Henry Tanner are more conventionally academic with their classical sources in the symmetrical former **Post Office**, 36-48 Waterloo Street, 1903-5; converted to offices, 1988.

C McKean

72**Distillers' Building**, 64 Waterloo Street, 1897, James Chalmers
Eclectic, in a quirky mix of Renaissance, Tudor and vague baronial. Note the seemingly truncated tower which ends in corbelled niches devoid of statuary but given barley sugar stick columns instead. Built for

Anne Dick

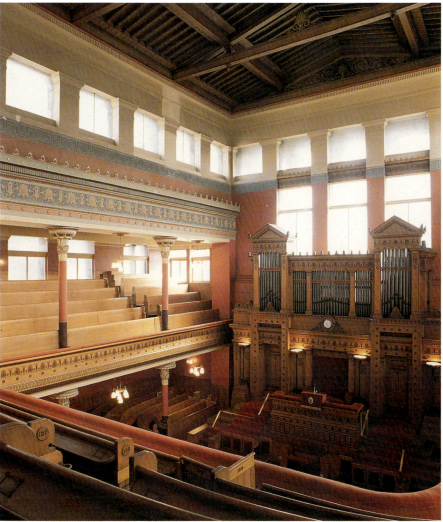

Interior and detail of the St Vincent Street Church by Alexander Thomson.

Right interior of the Library, the Glasgow School of Art. *Below* School of Art, west doorway. *Bottom* Room de Luxe, Willow Tea Rooms.

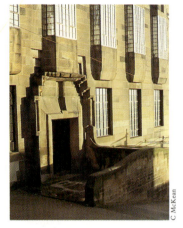

C McKean

Glasgow School of Art

Douglas MacGregor

Left the Willow Tea Rooms. *Below* Studio Drawing Room, Mackintosh House, Hunterian Art Gallery.

Douglas MacGregor

Hunterian Art Gallery

Left St George's Mansions. *Below* National Bank of Pakistan.

Anne Dick

Elder & Cannon

Left Waterloo Street in 1926 drawn by Robert Eadie. *Below* Distillers domeless.

distillers Wright & Greig, Rhoderick Dhu, not surprisingly, is one of the statues above the door.

Baltic Chambers, 40-60 Wellington Street, 1900, Duncan McNaughtan
Massive suite of offices with busy end-of-century Renaissance façades crowned at its splayed corners with splendid pagoda towers.

Popular Hotel, Holm Street, 1898-1901, F Burnet & Boston
Erected as the New Century Hotel for the city's 1901 Exhibition, it became a model lodging house after the Second World War, and is now deserted. A Chicago-like quality in its red sandstone façade undulates in shallow bays. A building worthy of a better fate.

Pacific House, 70 Wellington Street, 1984, Comprehensive Design.
Extensive commercial redevelopment in the 1960s and 1970s left the Holm anonymous and rather joyless, but some sense of place has now returned. Pacific House uses a splayed window theme in glass and brick to establish some formal relationships with older neighbours: with **Atlantic Chambers** (see p. 108) in Cadogan Street it does not quite work but the intention is admirable. Several buildings endorse the effort. King Main & Ellison are content to manipulate square bay slots of **Corunna House**, begun 1982. **Hanover House** on the corner of Cadogan Street and Douglas Street is more adventurous with canted bays, red brick buttress piers and a neat conservatory-like porch.

For bulk and bravura, the demolished Christian Institute, 1879, at 64-100 Bothwell Street was difficult to beat even in the rich context of Glasgow's Victorian architecture. It rose in a vigorous pile-up of gables and towers, variations on a round arch theme threaded through the rough weave of its street façade. Much of the money—and much was needed—to build it came from the Christian philanthropy of the Rutherglen chemical manufacturer James White and his son, the first Lord Overtoun. The Whites lived at Overtoun House, near Dumbarton, and it was perhaps for this reason that the Dumbarton architect John McLeod was given the commission. Two decades later, the YMCA to the west and the Bible Training Institute to the east were added by others. The BTI, as it was known, followed the training methods established by the American evangelist Moody (of Moody & Sankey fame), at Northfield, Connecticut, in commemoration of his visit to Glasgow in 1874.

Sauchiehall Street

Properly *Sauchie-haugh*—the meadow (haugh) of the willow trees (sauch)—Sauchiehall Street was no more than a winding lane from Swan's Yett (the head of Buchanan Street) to Clayslaps (Kelvingrove) until c.1807. Villas '*in nice gardens of an acre or so*' began to sprout, possibly attracted by Willowbank, 1807, the house of entrepreneur and *hotch-potch huxter* William Harley. Several short terraces of self-contained houses followed. In 1846, this *rural loaning* was widened to a continuous majestic street 60ft wide (which more than doubled land values), and in 1855 was extended through Charing Cross and the gardens of the Sandyford Terraces and then bent south-west to connect with Dumbarton Road. 'Senex' was amused by the new pretensions implied in the name Sauchiehall: *agreeably to the above mode of changing names, we may live to see the Flesher's Haugh changed to Flesher's Hall*. The ancient connection with willows was perpetuated by Miss Cranston in the Willow Tea Rooms.

Marks & Spencer, 1936

Mitchell Library

St Andrew House, 1964, Arthur Swift & Partners
A 15-storey tower block of aggregate panels superimposed on a long two-storey podium which replaced the Lyric Theatre, 1880, by James Thomson and Frank Matcham. Fashion changes: the design had many admirers at the time.

Empire House, 1964-5, Covell Matthews
Blue engineering bricks in an exposed concrete frame, over a two-storey podium. It commemorates the name, if not the magnificence, of Frank Matcham's 1897 Empire theatre.

British Home Stores,
1966, G W Clarke; William Nimmo
Plain, brick-cornered multiple store given a touch of style by its 1930-ish curved corner into Renfield Street.

Crown Rooms, 94-102 Sauchiehall Street,
1871, H K Bromhead
A severe if elegant building, formerly celebrated as the Aladdin's cave of Morrison & McChlery's auction rooms. Note the flamboyant sculpture above the steep flight of entrance steps, which led directly up to the first-floor rooms. Extended westward to the same design in yellow brick by Boyer & Partners, 1988.

Savoy Centre, 140 Sauchiehall Street, 1892-3, by H & D Barclay and its near neighbour at **204-208**, 1902, by Baird & Thomson, are both massive piles of busy classical detail, the former the stronger design with its bold arches with sculptured spandrels. Brash perhaps, but better value than the blank bare brick of Bradshaw, Rowse & Harker's **Sauchiehall Centre** with its meretricious Mackintosh plagiarism (a perverse replacement for the six-storeyed plate-glass splendour of Pettigrew & Stephens' department store which Mackintosh's own firm, Honeyman & Keppie, had built here in 1896-7). The free Renaissance frontage of **141-143**, 1904, is by Keppie.

At **Marks & Spencer**, 1936, the original bays are 1930s classic by Robert Lutyens.

73 **Willow Tea Rooms**, 1903-4, C R Mackintosh
The last of four such temples to temperance created for Kate Cranston. Carefully restored by the late Geoffrey Wimpenny, it now functions as a jewellery shop on the ground floor. The interior reveals all the spatial tricks and decorative delights of Mackintosh's genius. In the Room De-Luxe upstairs, itself a jewel glinting with silver, its mirrored slivers flashing, you

RIAS Library

can still sip tea. The tall, thin, white façade, with its square windows punched through walls, oversailing roof, and horizontal strip window foretells the 1930s. (Colour plate, p. 139)

Original drawing for the McLellan Galleries, from the *Building Chronicle*.

McLellan Galleries, 1855, James Smith
A long regular three-storey range built for coach maker, cathedral restorer and art buff Archibald McLellan, converted to house his bequest on his death; reserved and restrained but more urban than the terraces of Blythswood Hill. In 1904 Frank Burnet & Boston added the squat dome on the eastern corner (which collapsed in 1989) and in 1913-14 A B MacDonald's city architect's office the grand classical stairhall and galleries at the rear. *Tréron et Cie*, the shop that used to occupy the long street front, was the epitome of carriage-trade Glasgow with French rococo interiors.

1931 Bank of Scotland.

Bank of Scotland, 235 Sauchiehall Street,
1931, A Graham Henderson
Marks the corner of West Campbell Street with an austere ashlar box belted with a Greek fret frieze and topped off by a two-storeyed pilastered temple of offices. The sculpture is by Benno Schotz. From **269** all the way to Charing Cross, four-storey tenements over an almost uninterrupted series of bars and restaurants provide a strong, late classical, stone street wall.

74**Grecian Chambers, 336-356 Sauchiehall Street,**
1865, Alexander Thomson
A symmetrical range with a beautiful eaves gallery of squat Egyptian columns. The clarity of Thomson's design and the incised detail are sources of great

RIAS Collection

Top western Sauchiehall Street looking towards Charing Cross c. 1880. *Above* Grecian Chambers by Alexander Thomson. *Right* Charing Cross Mansions.

delight. Crisp and newly restored by Boswell, Mitchell & Johnston, even the shop fronts now bear Thomson's posthumous mark. Thomson's hand is probably also to be seen in the elegant shallow-relief tenement at **Nos 373-387**.

Craggy cliffs of red sandstone Burnet-inspired historicism designed by T L Watson and Henry Mitchell boost the scale at **Nos 396-450**, 1902-7.

Baird Hall, 1938, Weddell & Inglis
Built as the Beresford Hotel for the Empire
Exhibition, cinema-architect (and owner) Inglis gave
it a gigantic cinema façade to attract custom.
Formerly scarlet and black fins soar to ten storeys,
and the bulbous drum towers of bay windows were
capped by flagpoles. Despite the loss of much colour
and detail, it is still the highest and best of
Glasgow's 1930s architecture.

501 Sauchiehall Street, 1898, Robert Duncan
Surprisingly late version of the original 1855 Wylie
& Lochhead store on Buchanan Street: tall, florid red
sandstone, with elegant cast-iron mullions at the
windows.

518 Sauchiehall Street, 1904, John Keppie
Red sandstone, early Renaissance gable front with
Michaelangelesque figures to edify conservative
connoisseurs: appropriate for Glasgow's celebrated
photographers and Fine Art dealers, T & R Annan.
Note the new block opposite, corner of Elmbank
Street, 1988, by the Holmes Partnership. Although
the scale is held, the brick size fits uneasily beside
the great ashlar blocks, and the windowhead details
lack conviction.

National Bank of Pakistan,
1981-2, Elder & Cannon
Enigmatic, triangular patterned stone façade and
marbled door-surround open into a brilliantly lit
interior with Egyptian detail and mastery of spatial
effects.

75 **Charing Cross Mansions**,
1889-91, Burnet, Son & Campbell
A symbol of late 19th-century Glasgow. '*The Mairie
of the Charing Cross arrondissement*' according to Sir
John Summerson; a five-storey curve of rippling red
stone francophilia, flanked by taller, bay-windowed
pavilions and focused on a florid three-bay centrepiece with clock, carving and a galleried cupola.
The design bears study. Ground-floor shops were
originally intended to be glazed with the thinnest of
mullions. The two floors above are capped by a
balustraded balcony acting as cornice with arched
recessed attic storey above. Wonderfully French
dormer windows in roof. **Albany Chambers**, added
by Burnet six years later, extended the theme
eastwards along Sauchiehall Street concealing a late
Georgian mansion which still survives behind. The
same architects also extended around the corner to
the rather splendid **Nos 347-353 Renfrew Street**.

RIAS Collection

RCAHMS

Top Beresford Hotel (now Baird Hall)
when it opened. *Above* 518 Sauchiehall
Street.

145

Top left Breadalbane Terrace. *Top right* Peel Terrace both on Hill Street, Garnethill. *Right* the view across Sauchiehall Street from Garnethill to Blythswood Hill.

Tenement House, 1892

145 Buccleuch Street is in the most westerly of seven similar four-storey close units stretching from 71 Garnethill Street, a long stepping street block begun by the building firm of Ferguson & Anderson. In 1911, 25-year-old Agnes Toward and her mother moved into No 145, in which Agnes was to live most of her life. What makes the house unique is not its architectural distinction—it is typical rather than exceptional—but this long period of personal occupation by a Glasgow spinster who changed nothing in her home, surrounding herself with the accumulated trivia of a life-time. It is the furnishings and fittings of Miss Toward's flat, her personal 'treasures', letters and postcards, and mementoes, a veritable social history, which makes a visit to what has become the National Trust for Scotland's Tenement House perhaps the most intimate evocation of Edwardian life in Glasgow.

Open to the public: guidebook available

Right kitchen in the Tenement Flat.

76 **Peel Terrace**, Hill Street,
1841-2, possibly Charles Wilson
Along the crest, appropriately elevated, are some of
the city's finest tenements. Those in Peel Terrace are
high: four-storeyed, with an arcaded ground floor,
strong string courses and alternating pediments at
first floor. More exuberant still is Wilson's
Breadalbane Terrace, 1845-6, 1855-6, opposite,
enclosing the street from **97-113**: rhythmic
pediments, decorative consoles, a balustraded parapet
and balconied Roman Doric porches.

The red sandstone tenement ranges of the 1890s,
negotiating the slopes with canted bays, have real
street sense—especially those at **51-57 Rose Street**
77 and **105-145 Buccleuch Street**, 1891-3, by George
Bell II of Clarke & Bell. **145** is the National Trust
for Scotland's **Tenement House**.

Garnethill is not solely residential. There are two
churches, as different in architectural character as
religion. At the foot of West Graham Street, **Milton
Street Church**, 1849, by J Burnet, offers a modest
Gothic gable enlivened by open-traceried skews. The
red classical grandeur of **St Aloysius Church**, Rose
Street, 1908-10, by C J Menart follows the orthodox
Jesuit formula but adds a tall, judiciously swelling
campanile on the corner of Hill Street; a fine
concrete vaulted and domed interior conjures up a
vision of Italy for expatriates. Archibald
Macpherson's **St Aloysius College**, 1883, is tall and
refined, a Renaissance-style palazzo porched and
galleried at the centre, the projecting lower wings
added 1900-2. At the end of Hill Street, **Garnethill
Synagogue**, 1881, by John McLeod, '*one of the
oldest in Britain*', follows its own formal conventions,
instantly recognisable in a deeply revealed round
arched Romanesque portal. Unaltered interior,
marvellously evocative of times long past.

Of the several hospitals, the glazed Renfrew Street
façade of the **Dental Hospital**, 1931, by E G Wylie
is the best: steel frame evident in the chevron-
patterned blue spandrels, stone-enclosing façade plain
and well proportioned.

Garnet Hill School, Buccleuch Street,

1878, James Thomson
Broad and severe, with a central square tower and a
Roman Doric porch of coupled square columns.
Garnetbank school is red sandstone Renaissance at
231 Renfrew Street, by T L Watson, 1905.

Garnethill, the second but much
steeper hill over which the grid-
iron plan of Blythswood New
Town was spread, has always been
distinct. It was developed from
c.1820, as a leafier more suburban
quarter than the lands south of
Sauchiehall Street, '*dotted over with
detached self-contained residencies*'. A
few of these skew-gabled late
Georgian villas survive. All
small—three bays wide—and most
with columned porches. Mutilated
examples can be found on the
north side of Renfrew Street, but
the best are on the high ground:
Nos 120 (note its garden gate),
122, 125 and 135 Hill Street.

The earliest building on
Garnethill—or Summerhill as it
was first called—was the
Observatory opened in 1810 by the
Glasgow Astronomical Institution
on the brow of the hill. Anderson's
College played a major part in this
project, and its Professor of
Natural Philosophy, Thomas
Garnet, MD (1766-1806) was so
closely associated with the
observatory that he gave his name
to Garnethill. Although well-
equipped with instruments,
including a camera obscura and
solar microscope, the Observatory
did not survive the encroaching
smoke of industry beyond mid
century. Thomas de Quincey
visited it in the 1840s, and mused:
'*How tarnished with eternal canopies
of smoke, and of sorrow, how dark
with the agitations of many orders,
is the mighty town below! How
serene, how quiet, how lifted above
the confusion, and the roar, and the
strifes of earth, is the solemn
observatory that crowns the heights
overhead!*'

Right original perspective of the Cosmo Cinema. *Above* as first built.

School of Art entrance.

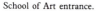

78 Glasgow Film Theatre,
1939, James McKissack & W J Anderson
Built at the corner of Rose Street and Renfrew Street, the Cosmo Cinema, as it was originally named, brought European films to the Glasgow public. In architectural character it was just as continental: deftly detailed brick and faience, well judged massing on its corner site and a stepped tower rising above the entrance—all suggest Dutch or Scandinavian influence. Fine entrance hall.

79 Glasgow School of Art, 167 Renfrew Street,
1897-99; 1907-9, C R Mackintosh
Mackintosh's masterwork. Won in a limited local competition in which every competitor warned that the brief could not be realised for the money available, the project took shape in two separate stages, although where the tall studio windows gather the light along Renfrew Street, or the towering castle walls climb up the hill to the south, it scarcely appears so. The gables betray the building's phased completion: in the east, the massy walls of a Scottish tower house; in the west, soaring gridded glass bays almost without precedent and certainly without parallel.

Tradition and innovation are the keys which unlock Mackintosh's genius. Contrast and conflict abound in an overall creative tension; filigree wrought-iron against gaunt ashlar or rubble; sinuous swirls and the rigorous waffle mesh of window patterns; nature and geometry; past and future.

Note particularly within: the toplit gallery at the head of the stairs; the Mackintosh Room to the east—magnificent furniture, fireplace and windows; the Museum, with its collection of Mackintosh material; and the Library—the two-storey galleried

Glasgow School of Art.

pièce de résistance of Celtic twilight—dark timber, filtering light, purples and shadows. (Colour plate, p. 138)

Coarse concrete crowds in on Mackintosh's masterpiece, with bruising Brutalist indifference. Gillespie Kidd & Coia's blue pedimented prefab, built in 1981 as a staff lounge, looking out across Renfrew Street into the Art School steps, is at least deferentially lightweight.

Royal Scottish Academy of Music & Drama, 1982-8, Sir Leslie Martin with Ivor Richards; William Nimmo & Partners

Royal Scottish Academy of Music and Drama.

Situated at the junction of Renfrew Street and Hope Street close to Scottish Opera's Theatre Royal (*q.v.*) and Scottish Television's studios and not far from the city's new Concert Hall (*q.v.*), the Academy bears all the conventional signs of cultural monumentality—pavement forecourt, grand entrance staircase, a scaled-up colonnade of finned brick piers. But in the gridded Glasgow streetscape it scarcely works, least of all in its specious peristyle and meaningless chamfered corner. Behind the façades, in a complex resolution of circulation, servicing and acoustic separation, lies a plan of masterly organisational clarity in which auditoria for Music School and Drama School are laterally wrapped by banks of practice rooms and teaching space.

149

William Stark's 1810 Lunatic Asylum (demolished).

Mitchell Library

St Stephen's Church.

Anne Dick

COWCADDENS

Glasgow's expansion north was minimal before 1800. Rottenrow and its westward extension as Love Loan marked the limit of built development. North and west lay the lands of Bell's Park and Little Cowcaddens, pitted with a series of building stone quarries (of which there were seven from the north end of St George's Road across the shoulder of Garnet Hill to the west end of what is now Cathedral Street). In 1790, Cracklinghouse Quarry, *a big affair*, was filled in and Dundas Street was opened over its site in 1812. In 1829 attempts were made to create a *Grand North Approach* but nothing was achieved until the setting out of Parliamentary Road.

Lunatic Asylum, 1810-14, William Stark
Supervised incarceration was the early 19th century's response to crime and madness alike. An achievement of genius, the asylum's saltire plan (based upon Ipswich Prison) comprised four, three-storeyed ward wings meeting in a higher hub containing day rooms, the whole crowned with an open Adam-inspired ribbed dome. Within a generation, Stark's solution was regarded as outmoded. The building survived as a poorhouse until its demolition in 1908.

80 **Dundas Vale Teachers' Centre**,
1836-7, David Hamilton
Thanks to the campaigning of educational reformer David Stow (1793-1864), Glasgow was the first city in Britain to build what he called a *Normal Seminary* for teacher training. Hamilton's elevations conform to Stow's desire they be '*the plainest possible*', though there is a porch of Roman Doric coupled columns and a classical clock-tower belfry rising above the staircase in the principal block at the heart of the U-plan. Wings are two-storeyed with round-headed windows and giant pilasters. Stow's later **Free**

Church Normal School, 1844-6 (dem.1973), by Thomas Burns, which stood nearby at 121 Cowcaddens, took a less ascetic view of style: its elevations, porch and belfry were dressed in castellated Gothic.

Victorian Cowcaddens, a densely packed inner suburb of tenements and factories, is wholly unrecognisable today. Comprehensive redevelopment in the 1960s and 1970s has transformed it into an anonymous zone of high-rise towers, balcony-access flats, curtain-wall office and college buildings of varying quality caught between the motorway and the more coherently Glaswegian townscape of the city centre to the south. Brick and ziggurat glass make their appearance in **Northgate House**, Milton Street, Stranded amid the doldrums, a few survivors still claim attention. At 30-34 McPhater Street **St Stephen's Parish Church**, 1872, by Campbell Douglas & Sellars, has a tattered Italianate dignity, which could yet be worthy of its site facing down Hope Street. More dramatically located at the gushet of Shamrock Street and New City Road, Neil Duff's **Trustee Savings Bank**, 1906, builds up a four-storeyed convex corner from a splendidly rich entrance to a balustraded Baroque dome. The high red brick box of **Stow College**, 1935, by James Miller, nearby, has modernist geometry reminiscent of the functional rigours of a Victorian mill.

Orient House, 16 McPhater Street, 1892-5, W J Anderson
Built first as workshops and warehousing but quickly extended and converted into a model lodging-house, this is a precociously *modern structure with partial steel framing, steel beams, and floors of reinforced concrete.* Yet the appeal is more than technical: various motifs drawn from Italian Renaissance precedent combine to evoke something of the fantasy world of the early picture house.

TSB, Cowcaddens.

Orient House.

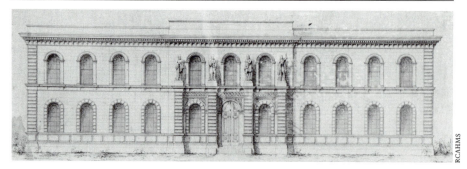

RCAHMS

Charles Wilson's elevation for Glasgow High School.

ELMBANK STREET

Nearer the Ring Road, most 19th-century buildings have been ripped out. It seems scarcely possible that India Street could ever have been one of the town's most charming residential streets, and one looks in vain for any trace of Elmbank Crescent. **Elmbank Street** has been a little luckier. On one side there is an incomplete and mutilated terrace from **11** to **27** and the appropriately Beaux-Arts baroque of **Scottish Opera Offices**, 1907 (originally the Institute of Shipbuilders), by J B Wilson. Opposite is the Italianate **Glasgow High School**, 1846-7, designed by Charles Wilson as Glasgow Academy—*a private school for young gentlemen*—and now one of many homes for Strathclyde Regional Council. Sculpted figures of Homer, Galileo, James Watt and Cicero look down on the street from elevated plinths above the entrance. J L Cowan's side wings, 1886-7, competently respectful of Wilson's style, are linked north and south by triumphal arch screens so that almost the entire eastern side of the street is taken up. Across the playground, the 1938-40 **Lodges** are by John Watson II, who also remodelled the rear of the original building.

Strathclyde Police Headquarters, Pitt Street, 1933, James Miller

Formerly the Commercial College, three storeys of neat red brick horizontality, with his customary squat entrance tower. On the other side of the block, facing west, more offices for the police concealed behind a waterfall of oblique glass which tumbles down into Holland Street. The stepped profile is a strange choice since it breaks the strongly vertical street walls of the neighbourhood.

SOUTH WOODSIDE

One of the city's most coherent enclaves of tenemented streets. Here the Glasgow grid was continued in the late 1830s by McHardy & Fullerton, solicitor entrepreneurs who developed

Inner Ring Motorway

Conceived in 1945 and still being built, the Inner Ring cuts a broad swathe of concrete, bridging and ditching around the north and west of the city centre. Much of the city's fabric which, judged by today's conservation conscience, might have been saved, was lost; and much that was overcrowded, insanitary and generally below standard had to go. It is a massive work of urban sculpture, a multi-track barrier that breached the continuity of Glasgow's townscape, a wound only now beginning to heal. The views are magnificent: north from Townhead to the canalside warehouses at Port Dundas, west to the ochre-towered skyline of Park, east onto the dramatically truncated streets of Garnet Hill, and—not least—from W A Fairhurst & Partners rather hefty **Kingston Bridge**, 1970, the prospect of the Clyde, upriver and down.

Woodlands Hill (see p. 156), but obliquely set off from St George's Road, filling the wedge-shaped stretch of land that lies between Woodlands Road and the die-straight boulevard line of Great Western Road.

81 **63-89 St George's Road**,
1900-1, Frank Burnet & Boston
At the flat angled corner of this wedge, designed to complement Charing Cross Mansions, the red bulwark of a pagoda-turetted tenement of real urban dignity. Tenements continue the wall down Woodlands Road but along St George's Road, scale and quality disintegrate. It was once altogether different: a short series of flanking mansions lined the road, their architecture, severely Georgian, their gardens generously planted.

Anne Dick

Queen's Crescent.

82 **Queen's Crescent**, from 1837, John Bryce
Two-storeyed arc of terrace houses rising at the ends and centre into three-storeyed flats, with Roman Doric porches, and pedimented first floor windows. To the north, where Melrose Street connects to Great Western Road, the composition has lost its balanced symmetry. To the south, however, across a semicircular garden with central fountain, Bryce's **Queen's Terrace**, 1850-2, closes the space with staid good taste. The eastern extension offers plain, late classical, three-storey houses with paired, pilastered porches. It begins the westward growth of **West Princes Street** parallel to Great Western Road.

C McKean

Until the 1870s, when a denser mesh of tenemented streets began to take shape, terraces appeared in intermittent speculation along the eastern and southern margins of the Woodside wedge. **7-11, 15-19** and **25 Ashley Street**, c. 1845, are the sole remnants; well endowed with window and pleasantly porched in fluted Ionic columns.

Stark and flat at first as in **Baliol Street** and **West End Park Street**, c.1850, most of the Woodside tenements have a characteristically undulating street façade of four-storeyed bows. **West Princes Street**, the backbone of the whole development, is notably consistent in scale and detail—and all the better for the changes in colour from ochre, through ochre-and-red polychromy, to red sandstone which, like the roof cone accents on corner bows, mark the gradual build-up of the street, c.1870-1900. Across this long quiet spine, run shorter ribs of four-storey tenements, several towards the west generously broad and filled with a central strip of tall trees.

Albany Academy, 44 Ashley Street, c. 1875, H & D Barclay
More like a city mansion than a school. John Burnet's **Arlington Baths**, 1871-5, run an uneasily arcaded façade down the west end of Arlington Street. The canted bays and grand frontispiece of the **Scottish Ballet Offices**, 1897, by George Bell all but disappear into the red sandstone wall of West Princes Street. Otherwise South Woodside is uncompromisingly residential: elegant, leafy and quiet, it is the finest of Glasgow's inner city suburbs.

St Silas Episcopal Church, 1864, John Honeyman
Three saddleback roofs in parallel, the higher nave, with a wheel window in its southern gable, pushing ahead of its five-bay flanking aisles. Inside is a fine timber roof diagonally braced and boarded. A pleasant lawn garth defined by Miles Gibson's 1895 Hall faces Park Road.

Queen's College, Park Drive, c. 1913, Walter R Watson
Safe red sandstone design, chosen in competition in which the assessors, as ever, steered clear of the Mackintosh entry. Lumpish with pleasing detail.

Woodlands St Jude's Church, Woodlands Road, 1874-5, John Burnet
Vigorous, soaring steepled Gothic, its washing revealing glorious orange stone: much inspired by elements from the unsuccessful competition entrants for which Burnet had been the assessor.

West Princes Street.

RCAHMS

Top West End Park Street, with new tenement by ASSIST on left. *Above* Woodlands St Jude's Church. *Middle left* Arlington Baths. *Left* typical tenement square.

Woodside School, 1881-2, Robert Dalglish
Outside the wedge, at the west end of Woodlands Road, this competition-winning design is an exercise in restrained English Jacobean, two tall storeys crested with open stonework parapets. The plainer north-west block was added in 1896.

Woodside Place c. 1850.

Mitchell Library

The elegant terraces which now lie to the west of Charing Cross were built on land feued from the Campbells, first for country houses: Wellfield, Woodlands and Clairmont House. Although none survives, the line of Claremont Street follows that of the gated drive which Hugh Cross of Clairmont laid up to his mansion. The building of terraces, spaciously set and generously planted with trees, began in the 1820s with Crescent Place, now gone like the **Grand Hotel**, 1877, by James Thomson which later concealed it.

Below Elderslie Street.

C McKean

WOODLANDS

During the second half of the 18th century, much of the Campbell land that stretched from Woodlands Hill to the Kelvin was feued off for several new estates, varying greatly in size, each demesne with its own mansion. Most lasted under a century. The finest was **Kelvingrove House**, begun c.1783, and enlarged in the 1790s, by David Hamilton. Commissioned by Lord Provost Patrick Colquhoun as a mansion fit for the city's leading citizen, its design combined the elements of late Roman classicism in an original *'almost whimsical'* way. **Kelvingrove**, c.1788 and demolished in c.1875, was a modest skew-gabled property, on ground which today serves as the bowling green in Kelvingrove Park. On Woodlands Hill, James McNayr, editor of the *Glasgow Herald*, built **Woodlands House** in 1802, called 'McNayr's Folly', since its location was still at that time regarded as an *'out of the way place from which to pursue business in the city'*. Out of the way or not, Woodlands Hill was soon to become the third of Glasgow's drumlins to be developed. In less than a generation, the West End estates—23 in all, covering some 1250 acres east and west of the Kelvin—begin to transform themselves into building sites *'with magical rapidity'*. South Woodside was first to go, terraces spreading out along the line of Sauchiehall Road and up to the eastern slopes of Woodlands Hill.

83**Woodside Crescent**, 1831, George Smith
The crescent was the first of these wonderful, yellow sandstone Grecian terraces, sweeping up Woodlands Hill in a strong concave curve, punctuated with Doric porches. The scale rises to three storeys in the straight-cut severity of **Woodside Terrace**, 1835. **Woodside Place**, 1838, below the gardens, runs

Anne Dick

David Leslie

David Leslie

Above West
Princes Street.
Left caryatids
from St
Andrew's Halls.

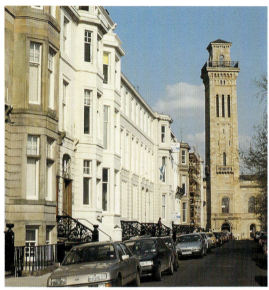

Left Woodlands Terrace. *Below* the Henry Wood Hall.

C. McKean

Jack Notman

Top Old Partick Bridge painted by William Dale in 1868, from a viewpoint about the Bishop's Mill. *Right* The Ship Launch, Barclay-Curle Yard, Stobcross, in the 1830s.

Above the skyline of Park. *Right and far right* Park Circus and its towers from Glasgow University.

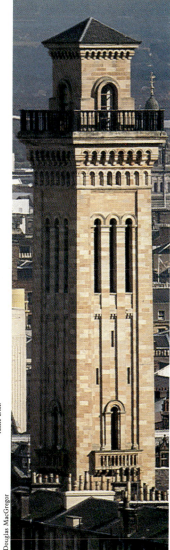

C McKean

C McKean

FAR LEFT St Vincent Crescent
(above); Minerva Street (below).

This page above the Main Hall, the
Glasgow International Exhibition, 1901,
painted by William Kennedy. *Left*
Glasgow Art Gallery and Museum —
the Natural History Gallery and East
Staircase.

C McKean

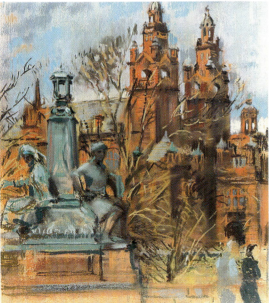

A Alexander

Left Lynedoch Crescent c. 1850. *Below* Claremont Terrace. *Bottom* Claremont Terrace when first built.

parallel backing Newton Place. Woodside Place has an extra storey in height forming centre and end pavilions in best New Town style. The Doric doorways are huge and splendid. All three terraces were designed by Aberdeen-born, Edinburgh architect George Smith for entrepreneurial solicitors McHardy & Fullarton, and were for sale at extraordinarily high cost. Smith continued the residential advance uphill with **Lynedoch Street**, and **Lynedoch Crescent**, both c.1845, in similar (if softer) classical vein.

Claremont House, c.1835, John Baird I
Set the style of Baird's **Claremont Terrace** which was added on both sides between 1842-7; a shallow three-storey ashlar crescent with protruberant porches and splendid balcony ironwork. Across a delightful sylvan glade (maintained as the private preserve of residents) **Claremont Gardens** appeared in 1857; more Victorian in its classicism with consoled tripartite doorways and ogee corbelled bays—possibly the work of Charles Wilson.

C McKean

Park Gate.

The view from Park over to the Docks.

RCAHMS

Park, 1855-63, Charles Wilson
A magnificent contoured ring of French-roofed terraces dominate the green valley of the Kelvin below, enlivening the city skyline for miles around.

Residential development followed the abandonment of John Baird and Edward Blore's 1846-9 plans to relocate the University here. Looking out over the West End like inhabited ramparts, vigorously modelled in façade and roof, **Park Terrace**, 1855, and **Park Quadrant**, 1855-8, protect the calmer, 84 almost aristocratic, elegance of **Park Circus**, 1857-63, within. It is Wilson's finest achievement, a piece of townscape unsurpassed in Glasgow for subtle classical reserve. Most houses have columned entrance halls, rich plaster work and splendid marble chimneypieces. The monumental granite stairway of Woodlands Terrace was added in 1853 by Charles Wilson at the extraordinary cost of £10,000. The magnificent equestrian bronze is the **Roberts Memorial**, 1915, by Harry Bates. (Colour plate, p. 182)

22 Park Circus, redecorated 1899,
James Salmon (Jun) & J Gaff Gillespie
Some of the best Glasgow Style finish added to an already lavish palazzo interior which James Boucher had created in 1872 for Walter Macfarlane of the Saracen Foundry (hence cast-iron pavilion at rear).

85 **Trinity College**, 1856-61, Charles Wilson
Park would be less splendid were it not for its four tall towers, vertical foils to the horizontality of terraced houses, like a Scottish San Gimignano. Three of the towers, rising like Romanesque belfries, belong to Trinity College, formerly the Free Church College, now imaginatively converted to flats by James Cunning, Young & Partners. The fiercely finialled fourth is that of **Park Parish Church**, 1856-7, by J T Rochead, bereft of its gablet-clerestoried nave (dem. 1969) but not entirely ill served by the splayed bays and roofs of 1970 offices by Derek Stephenson clustered round buttressed base.

86 **Queen's Rooms**, La Belle Place,
1857-8, Charles Wilson
A huge Italian Renaissance ashlar box, now Christian Science Church, built to house a suite of assembly rooms and a concert hall to serve the social needs of the new community. Pedimented and temple-like, yet solid rather than columned, its deep frieze was richly carved by John Mossman. **2-5 La Belle Place**, 1856-7, also by Wilson, is a short run of tenements, surprisingly rich in decorative floral and shell motifs and grand details within. Possibly the first Glasgow tenements to have canted bay windows.

C McKean

University of Glasgow

C McKean

Top Park with the University,
Kelvingrove and Partick in the distance.
Above left John Baird's unsuccessful
proposal for Glasgow University. *Above
right* Park Circus.

SAUCHIEHALL STREET

Right Queen's Rooms, with adjacent tenement. *Below* Sandyford Place. *Middle right* Somerset Place. *Bottom right* Royal Crescent. Note that Sauchiehall Street had not yet been blasted through the gardens between Royal Crescent and Fitzroy Place, and that Claremont leads off into undeveloped countryside. *Bottom left* Kelvingrove Street.

Anne Dick

C McKean

C McKean

C McKean

87 **Newton Place**, Sauchiehall Street,
1837, George Smith
Part of Smith's development for McHardy &
Fullarton. A long run of 27 houses, raised at the
ends and in the centre in the characteristic manner of
the Blythswood new town, its cool reserve and bowed
ironwork balconies make it still one of the finest in
the inner west end. For almost a straight half-mile,
Sauchiehall Street was lined with similar housing, at
once urbane and urban. On the south side, **Newton
Terrace**, 1864-5, shorter but higher than its
namesake opposite, **Sandyford Place**, 1842-56, by
Brown & Carrick, and **Fitzroy Place**, 1847, by J
Burnet, running on in into **Westminster Terrace**,
1854. On the north, John Baird I followed the model
of Newton Place in **Somerset Place**, 1840, but in
grander style with consoled doorways and a
balustraded parapet. **Clifton Place**, originally
similar, was redeveloped in 1970 in to what was then
considered modern classicism.

88 **Royal Crescent**, 1839, Alexander Taylor
'*A pretty specimen of the dwellings of the better classes
in Glasgow.*' The unity of the crescent is maintained
by repetition, with emphasis at the ends and centre.
Yet each house receives an individual street façade,
not just in the coupled Ionic porches, but by some
particular elaboration of consoles, pediment or
chimney. Impressively tall and austere book-end
pavilions have giant order pilasters and attic storeys
recalling the Adams' College Buildings on the High
Street (see p. 27), though in a flatter, less academic
sense. The western pavilion takes a bold bowed curve
into the tenements of Kelvingrove Street.

89 **Kelvingrove Parish Church**, Derby Street,
1878-80, Campbell Douglas & Sellars
One of James Sellars' finest buildings: an austere
Greek classical temple, entered through a
pedimented, Ionic-columned eastern portico.
Curiously fretted cupola above. Now a recording
studio. It dominates a small square facing
Kelvingrove Street, in which Kelvingrove UP
Church, a Sainte Chapelle by Robert Baldie, 1878,
had stood until burnt in 1925.

Apsley Hotel, 901-903 Sauchiehall Street,
1853, Charles Wilson.
Designed originally as flats, it presents an Italianate
palazzo corner with fine floral frieze and consoled
cornice; and sets a good pattern for the rest of the
block.

Kelvingrove Parish Church.

C McKean

169

Above Henry Wood Hall. *Above right* the façade of St Andrew's Halls. *Below* Berkeley Street.

Berkeley Street, 1858-60
Nos 53-91 and **48-82** form pleasantly classical two-storey terraces, smaller than those facing Sauchiehall Street. Tenements in Berkeley Street are plain but absorb an exotic intrusion of brick baronial at **138**. The skin-deep casino façade at 34 Berkeley Street is no more than a bricked-up travesty of the former 1961 **Highlanders' Institute** which closed in 1979. The Institute had a concave 1950s façade of marble and facing brick, flanked by flag-poles and spattered generously with framed windows; itself a conversion concealing the original gabled front of the United Presbyterian Church, 1856, by John Burnet.

90 **Mitchell Library**, 1906-11, W B Whitie
There is no denying the floodlit Renaissance drama of Whitie's competition-winning façade and dome, with sumptuous interiors and marble stairs to match. Sir Frank Mears & Partners enlarged the library and archives 1972-81, enclosing the block with immensely heavy lateral walls of gridded ashlar. The *Glasgow Room* within is an unequalled treasure-chest of material about the City.

St Andrew's Halls, 1873-7, James Sellars
The west façade of the Mitchell Library represents all that remains of the city's once celebrated concert hall after the disastrous fire of 1962. Originally built for a private company of wealthy west-enders for whom the City Hall was no longer sufficiently grand or large, there is no more masterly nor more powerful classical façade in the city. Note the caryatids; plentiful sculpture by the Mossmans (Colour plate, p. 157). Superb range of 1850s classical tenements or warehouses in **North Street**, with giant channelled pilasters and conches. New glazed book-end with corner tower at the bottom by Jenkins & Marr.

Wylie & Lochhead's Factory, Kent Road,
1879, James Sellars
Converted to flats, its third-floor thermal semicircular windows must make unique rooms. It was
also Sellars who filled the city block at **97-113
Berkeley Street**, 1873, for John Wylie, this time as
a hire establishment. With its higher piended
pavilions at the four corners, it looks like the
misplaced provincial *schloss* of some minor Austrian
Count. Elegant glazed riding school within.

91 **Henry Wood Hall**, 1863-4, John Honeyman
The buttressed broach spire of the former Trinity
Congregational Church marks the corner of Berkeley
Street and Claremont Street. The building was
converted by Jack Notman for use by the Scottish
National Orchestra in 1978, providing a tall, well-lit,
T-plan rehearsal space. Fine window tracery in the
gables. (Colour plate, p. 160)

RCAHMS

Anderston Centre, Argyle Street,
1972, Richard Seifert & Partners
All the confidence of comprehensive
redevelopment—multi-level shopping, multi-storey
living, offices, car parking, a bus station. The high-
rise flats are still occupied, the cars and buses come
and go; but there is none of the hoped-for market-
place excitement. Escalators lie idle and the raised
level of what was planned as a busy shopping plaza
has turned into a bleak Business Centre, deserted and
still but for the somehow sinister blink of VDUs and
the bored glances of lonely secretaries. It was just a
few hundred yards too far west.

Buttery, 650 Argyle Street
A single corner tenement, surviving like a molar in a
caries-ridden jaw—more splendid for its bar and
restaurant, one suspects, than any other distinction.
Its location will soon make more sense with a street
of tenements by Simister Monaghan.

As Glasgow moved west, it
absorbed the small village of
Grahamston (where Argyle Street
stretched out past its link south
across the river at Jamaica Street).
West lay the Stobcross Estate
owned by the Anderson family
since the 16th century. In 1725
James Anderson had begun the
new village of Anderston close to
the Gushet Farm (later Anderston
Cross and now the expressway
bridge). When the estate passed to
John Orr of Barrowfield in 1735,
weavers' cottages lined both sides
of Anderston's Main Street, there
were bleachfields by the river and a
handful of isolated mansions
enjoying the riparian countryside.
Orr established Finnieston,
adjacent, in 1768, naming it after
his chaplain. By 1800 it was a
thriving little community, brewing
and glass-making augmenting the
prosperity of the textile industry.
An independent burgh in 1824, it
turned to heavy industry and was
swelled by Irish immigration
spilling up from the Broomielaw. It
was absorbed by Glasgow in 1846.

Anderston Centre Glasgow's answer to
London's London Wall.

Stobcross House
The residence of James Anderson,
built in 1696, stood near the
Exhibition Centre railway station.
'*A convenient house, sited upon
eminence above the river, with
suitable gardens, and avenue to the
water*', it was a wide, crow-stepped
mansion, decidedly Scottish in
form and detail, despite 18th- and
19th-century additions. By 1820 it
was '*in a decadent state*'. The
Victorian transformation of much
of Stobcross Estate into a middle-
class suburb developed along the
undulating line of St Vincent
Crescent—'*the first crescent erected
in Glasgow and subdivided into flats,
to which the advantage of pleasure
grounds has been attached*'—
impaired its setting. When the
docks were cut, its days were
numbered.

92 Savings Bank, 752 Argyle Street, 1899-1900, James Salmon
A *tour de force* alive with the attenuated sculptural motifs of the Glasgow Style by Albert Hodge and Johaan Keller. Tall, slender, blushing pink and turreted, with wonderful stiff-leaf carved armorial panel.

392-448 St Vincent Street,
1983-6, James Cunning, Cunningham & Associates
One of the first successful modern attempts to match the street sense of the tenements, although lower and facing a wider road. Strongly modelled with oriel windows in orange brick, its massive ends are crude by comparison.

Across the street 9-, 11- and 13-storey slabs of SSHA housing define the edge of the new comprehensively redeveloped Anderston like prison walls. The huge, rather unsubtle, copper pyramid of **Anderston Kelvingrove Church**, 1967-8, by Honeyman, Jack & Robertson relieves the square-cut monotony. Pugin & Pugin's standard model red sandstone Gothic **St Patrick's Church**, 1896-8, built on the site of the old Blythswood Foundry on North Street, has well-carved details and good tracery in its seven-light decorated east window. Round the corner in William Street, the rough little gabled box of **St Matthew's School**, 1846, survives as a nursery.

Some more recent housing makes an occasional if modest impression; the balconied dormers on **Houldsworth Street** and **Elliot Street**, 1987-8, by J B Hopton Associates are tricky but hardly urban.

Top armorial panel from James Salmon's Savings Bank. *Above* the new houses lining St Vincent Street. *Below right* Clydeway Industrial Centre.

Clydeway Industrial Centre,
1968-70, Jack Holmes & Partners
Six-tier cake of russet brick and concrete. Robust, even vulgar, its forceful warehousing bulk has a peculiarly Glaswegian impact.

Parr Partnership

FINNIESTON

Alexander Kirkland, 1824-92 began his intriguing career as both architect and engineer for James Scott's developments in Bothwell Street and at Stobcross. At 4-26 Bothwell Street (see p. 134) he seems to have collaborated, in matters of architectural style at least, with John Bryce. If similarity of detail is anything to judge by, Bryce's hand may also have been at work in St Vincent Crescent. For his now demolished Venetian warehouse in Miller Street and the precariously extant Eagle Buildings, Bothwell Street (see p. 136), his partner was James Russell (though the real designer in each case may well have been his assistant James Hamilton).

Despite a large and apparently successful practice, he left Glasgow suddenly in 1861. After a spell in London he emigrated to America to settle in Chicago in 1871. He became Commissioner for Public Buildings and designed the County Buildings jointly with J J Egan, in 1891. Kirkland may have played a part in the emergence in Chicago of what Louis Sullivan called '*The Tall Office Building Artistically Considered*'.

Queen's Dock, 1882, James Deas
The opening of Queen's Dock and the railway spelt the end of Stobcross House and Finnieston. Cut and built in Giffnock stone, the Dock transformed the area into a city service centre, legacies of which are still evident. It was filled for the Scottish Exhibition Centre (see below). Only the **Finnieston Crane**, 1932, by Cowans Sheldon, now recalls the mercantile bustle. The crane could load railway engines and tanks on to cargo ships, which is said to be one reason for its survival. Otherwise, the engineering works have gone. Anderston Walk and Main Street, once absorbed into Argyle Street, are now severed by the motorway.

Scottish Exhibition & Conference Centre, 1984, James Parr & Partners
Red and grey wriggly metal glandular volumes flanking a central, top-lit atrium, created upon the Queen's Dock to contain party-political conferences, prestigious trade exhibitions, concerts, and the annual Carnival. **Forum Hotel** by Cobban & Lironi, 1989, is a tall, staggered blue-glass tower, with a large white podium.

Pumphouse Complex, Stobcross Quay, 1877-8, John Carrick
Fine ashlar box with Italianate campanile restored and extended, after years of neglect, to a restaurant complex in 1988 by the Miller Partnership.

Minerva Street, 1853-6
Bends powerfully into Argyle Street in a convex tenemented range, originally reflected in a similar but shorter curving corner opposite. Above an arcaded ground floor, giant Corinthian pilasters mark the sweep of the corner. The four-storeyed street wall beyond runs south in regular repetitive rhythm.
Corunna Street, 1851-8, retains its symmetrical junction with Argyle Street in balanced bow-cornered tenements.

Left Scottish Exhibition Centre. *Below* Minerva Street corner.

C McKean

Above St Vincent Crescent in the 1850s, partially complete.

93 St Vincent Crescent, 1849-58, Alexander Kirkland
The most outstanding late classical terrace in Scotland; almost half a mile of main door and common stair flats, with Roman Doric porches and balustraded eaves. Its regular rhythms seem almost to be on the move, '*not unlike a very long passenger train on a double reverse curve*'. The prospect south is no longer a green riverside idyll—though the 1860 cast-iron columned gate to the bowling green survives.

Kelvinhaugh Street,
1987-8, Cooper Cromar Associates
Long terrace of student housing planned to swing round a public piazza into the west end of St Vincent Crescent; gables advance and recede in a Post-Modernist wall of brick polychromy. **Franklin Terrace**, 1171-1263 Argyle Street, c.1850 is revealed in glowing stone and good glazing bars—previously celebrated for its lone, contemporary tree and immense longitude.

Sandyford Henderson Memorial Church,
1854-6, J T Emmett
Buttressed front of three gables, each with delicate cinquefoil tracery, completed by John Honeyman.

Pearson Hall, Yorkhill Street,
1900-1, Leiper & McNab
Built as Battalion Headquarters for the Highland Light Infantry, and now used by the Parachute Regiment (TA). Offices, stairs and drill-hall gable pack together in overlapping splays and curves in polychromatic sandstone and brick—red, pink and ochre. Leiper has created a fortress-workshop, marking one entrance with a slot of tiered bay windows, the other with a powerfully swollen banded drum, each embedded obliquely into the street façade.

Below scheme by Cooper Cromar for the gushet of Sauchiehall Street and Dumbarton Road.

Partick

An ancient village built around mills on the Kelvin. As a reward for their help in the battle of Langside in 1569, the Incorporation of Bakers in Glasgow were granted the rights to a mill variously known as Regent's Mill (after the Regent Moray, victor of Langside), Archbishop's Mill (presumably in recognition of the original church licensees), and Bunhouse Mill (after a nearby tavern called the Bun and Yill House). Mills and villages were clustered around old Partick Bridge, erected in 1577 by Captain Thomas Crawford of Jordanhill. The mill-based economy gave way to industrial employment in the 19th century: rustic cottages replaced by streets and tenements.

94 **Bishop's Mill**, 1839 and 1853
Plain and noble four-storey, 10-bay, dressed rubble mill with raised polished margins, and distinctive for the wheatsheaves which surmount the gables. Often mistaken for chimney-stacks, they served only as a symbol of the building's function. The tail-race which ran in front of the building was filled during the building's recent conversion to housing, although the mark of the mill-wheel is still clearly incised.

95 **Glasgow Transport Museum**,
1929, Thomas Somers
Built as the Kelvin Hall on the site of the former Bunhouse Mill, it consists of a decorated, truly massive front, with towers, domes and somewhat fascist colonnade concealing two sheds behind. Towers and door details are American Jazz-Modern. Converted and cleaned, the building now encloses track and sports facilities, and the City's new Transport Museum.

Anderson College of Medicine, Dumbarton Road, 1888, James Sellars
Sellars dying from an infected foot injury (sustained when on a Highland walking holiday), completion of

Partick Castle

Lo Partick Castle, drear and lone,
Stands like a silent looker-on,
Where Clyde and Kelvin meet.

Legend has it that the medieval Bishop's Manor stood at the junction of the rivers. But the verse refers to the ruins of the 1611 L-plan tower designed by mason William Miller for George Hutcheson, joint founder of Hutchesons' Hospital (see p. 73). The unit of measurement was the length of *ye said George's ain fute*. Laid out with gardens and orchards, its meadowland setting remained unspoiled for the next two centuries, until finally demolished in the mid-19th century. Its site is near the current railway bridge.

Left Partick Bridge in 1850. *Below* the mills of Partick, Bishop's Mill on the right, Glasgow University spire in the distance.

Matheson Gleave

Keppie Henderson

Top Queen Mother's Hospital. *Above* the Western Infirmary.

Yorkhill, the first significant habitation on the superb wooded hill overlooking the confluence of the Clyde and Kelvin, was a Roman fort of the second century AD. In the 1830s, the painter Graham Gilbert bought an 1805 mansion and lived there until his death in 1866. The house was demolished, the land subdivided and feued for tenements. Some street names recall the former estates of Yorkhill and Over Newton. Lumsden and Blackie Streets commemorate two Provosts of the period. Mid century brought Yorkhill Station, on the City & District Railway, and Yorkhill Wharf with a huge timber depot adjoining.

the college fell to John Keppie: a sandstone, early Italian Renaissance composition whose sculpted tympanum is a major work by Pittendrigh Macgillivray.

Tennent Memorial Institute, Church Street, 1935, Norman A Dick
The Infirmary's Eye Department presents a plain stone face to the outside, relieved by the profusion of sculpture with flanking, crouched, figures by Archibald Dawson around the doorpiece. T Harold Hughes's scheme to make it the centrepiece of a larger composition has remained only half executed.

Queen Mother's Hospital, 1964, J L Gleave & Partners
Tower-and-podium of crisp utility but doubtful delight, well exemplifying the brisk attitude of the time. You were expected to be able to read the building from the outside: staircase tower, wards, utility rooms and bedrooms all clearly identified. The **Royal Hospital for Sick Children**, by Baxter Clark & Paul, 1971, by contrast is more composed, and therefore less legible: the dark block at the core contrasts with white, horizontal banding of each floor.

96 **Western Infirmary**, 1871-4, John Burnet (sen)
Immense H-plan Scots baronial hospital, without the Flemish Gothic elements which enliven the bulk of the University on the adjacent hilltop. Main block partly demolished. Pepper-pot turrets on the Glamis Castle model abound on the central entrance block, which contained theatre and lecture rooms. Nine ward blocks sprout on either side, and corbie-stepped gables ennoble the wings. The Pathology Block added by J J Burnet in 1894, and the Out-Patient and Boiler House facilities, crow-stepped gables to Church Street, in 1913.

Main Ward Block, 1974, Keppie Henderson & Partners
Housing accident and emergency facilities, this presents 11 storeys of contrasted engineering brick base, and the white striped horizontality of its pre-cast balcony facings. Its still vivid whiteness results from the incorporation of a high proportion of white Skye marble. The Nurses' Training School to the north also by Keppie Henderson. The **Nurses' Home**, by the Kelvin, stylish L-shaped with curved corners, corner windows and other 1930s details, was designed pre-war by Norman Dick and completed in 1948; style somewhat masked by the use of grey stone.

Hunterian Museum

C. McKean

Kelvingrove

The first use of the name Kelvingrove to describe the 24 acres of Glasgow's West End park occurs after the purchase of the property by Patrick Colquhoun in 1782. In 1852, the Corporation bought estate, mansion and woodlands for a public park (later increased by the acquisition of Clayslaps from the University). The few buildings, monuments, fountains, and bridges currently in Kelvingrove all derive from Glasgow's curious history of Great Exhibitions held on this site. The first **Glasgow Exhibition** was held in an atmosphere of High Victorian optimism in 1888, housed in spectacularly oriental Exhibition Halls designed by James Sellars. Displays ranged from lacemaking to shipbuilding, international displays in the main building including an Indian Street, populated by Indians, and a full size replica of the Bishop's Castle tower. It produced a clear profit and an architectural competition was held in 1891 to design a new Art Gallery and Museum for the City, to be paid for with the surplus.

Top left Kelvingrove House as drawn by David Hamilton. *Left* the original entrance front of Kelvingrove Art Gallery.

James Bridie's 'Serenata' to the West End Park (Kelvingrove) requires to be sung, with a Kelvinside accent, to the negro spiritual 'Nancy Till'.

> It's long pest midnight, there's
>   no one in the street,
> The constable is sleeping at the
>   corner of his beat.
> The cold white erc-lamps fizz
>   like gingerade,
> And I'm below your window
>   with this cherming serenade.
> Open your window the nicht is
>   beastly dark,
> The phentoms are dencing in
>   the West-End Park,
> Open your window, your lover
>   brave to see,
> I'm here all alone, and there's
>   no-one here but me!

97 **Kelvingrove Art Gallery & Museum**, 1901, Sir J W Simpson & Milner Allen Won in competition, against stiff local challenge: the design reflects the taste of the English assessor Alfred Waterhouse. All the self-assurance of the period which produced it: red Renaissance, its huge bulk embellished by fine New Sculpture by Sir George Frampton and others. Galleries sprout east and west from the great, high-roofed, hall which runs from front to back, framed by twin towers facing the University. Suits of armour vie with stuffed animal displays, treasures from Egypt and prehistoric remains. Upper galleries contain the City's international collection of Impressionist paintings. Other galleries contain significant Dutch and Italian

The 1901 Exhibition, designed mainly by James Miller, celebrated the continuing industrial prosperity of Glasgow (and the opening of its magnificent Art Gallery) with three huge buildings: the Industrial Hall, Machinery Hall and the Concert Hall. There were extravagant Russian timber buildings by Shekhtel. Only the Sunlight Cottages survive, based on the housing blocks at Port Sunlight, Cheshire: brick with Elizabethan-style half-timbering on the upper level. So untypical of Glaswegian workers' housing, they would have been regarded simply as one of many 'foreign' exhibits. The **1911 Exhibition** was to raise funds for a new Chair of Scottish History and Literature at Glasgow University. The architecture by R J Walker (who had assisted Miller in 1901) was consequently of a Scottish timber with baronial exhibition and concert halls.

Renaissance paintings, and the City's best-known modern painting, Dali's *Christ of St John on the Cross*. On the upper gallery can be seen Mossman's fine marble head of Alexander Thomson. Legend has it that the Gallery was built back to front and the architect jumped from the tower: wonderful legend, poor history: very Glaswegian.

RJAS Library

Mitchell Library

Above the extravagant 1901 pavilion by James Miller in Kelvingrove. *Right* Stewart Fountain. Note how small the trees are.

Gilmorehill

The lands occupied by the University of Glasgow have been known as Gilmorehill since the 17th century. It was owned by a succession of West Indian merchants, one of whom, Robert Bogel, built a fine new mansion in the style of David Hamilton in 1802. In 1845, Gilmorehill was sold to the Glasgow Western Cemetery Company, which proposed a rural Necropolis for the wealthy citizenry. Fortunately the Company predeceased any implementation of its purpose, and in 1865, Gilmorehill was bought by the College of Glasgow.

98**Stewart Fountain**, 1872, James Sellars
Gloriously restored, splashy, French Gothic fountain in the style of William Burges. A work of celebratory sculpture, it is the centrepiece of Park's eastern limb. Sculpture by Mossman. The fountain commemorates Lord Provost Stewart who was largely responsible for devising the city's water supply from Loch Katrine. The nearby 1894 Prince of Wales Bridge is large, opulent and worth a look. Other good statuary includes the 1913 Monument to Lord Kelvin by A M Shannan, and the bronze tiger group, 1866, by A Cain, and cast in Paris.

99 **Glasgow University**, Gilmorehill,
1866-86, Sir George Gilbert Scott
One of Scott's finest buildings. It is dominated by
the ghost of the Old College—a similar plan of two
quadrangles (inherited from an earlier scheme by
John Baird, for Woodlands Hills), albeit greatly
extended and attenuated, and a skyline of turreted
corner towers. The massively crowstepped pavilions
which flank the long south façade are based upon
Glasgow Cathedral chapter house. The University's
most recognised feature, the soaring Flemish
ventilation tower at the centre of the south front, its
spire a substitution by J O Scott for his father's solid
one, acts as a focus in much the same way that the
old Dutch steeple had done in the High Street.
There is a thoroughgoing homogeneity about the
design, based upon Scott's desire for an appropriate
architecture for the task: '*a style which I may call my
own invention, having already introduced it at the
Albert Institute in Dundee. It is simply a 13th- or 14th-
century secular style with the addition of certain
Scottish features peculiar to that country in the 16th
century.*'

Above Glasgow University floodlit in
1951. *Below* the University etched by J
Paterson; *below left* the Hunterian
Museum and Memorial Gates etched by
Wilfred Appleby (both by courtesy of
the Hunterian Museum).

Above the Lion and Unicorn staircase, as relocated, etched by J Thomson in 1913. Note Kelvingrove towers in the distance. *Right* original proposal for the Bute Hall.

Hunterian Museum

RIBA Library

Professors' Square.

Neil Baxter

For all its historicism, the building was thoroughly modern in plan and construction: extensive public use of iron in the western museum hall, the Library (now divided), and the Bute Hall. The **Hunterian Museum** (the oldest museum in Scotland, being in existence prior to 1796) projects a bulbous, two-tiered, five-windowed apse as a central focus of the north façade. With its graceful stone arcades and open timber roof, it is a fine example of Victorian medievalism. The **Bute Hall**—another piece of patronage by the Marquess in 1878—forms together with the Randolph Hall a superb focus for the entire University. A five-bay, aisled and galleried Hall, sitting upon an open, rib-vaulted undercroft, its exterior is defined by buttresses, traceried windows and circular towers. The tall, clustered columns stencilled with fleur-de-lys in Bute blue and gold colours are nonetheless of iron. (Colour plate opposite). The **Randolph Hall** contains magnificent windows by Morris and Burne Jones and by Douglas Strachan. The Senate Room contains panelling, a fireplace, and some furniture from the Fore Hall, Old College.

Lion and Unicorn Stair, 1690, William Riddel Stair and doorway which led up to the Fore Hall at the Old College (Colour page 11), re-erected back to front against the West Range. The range itself was

Right The Bute Hall, *Below* Glasgow University and Gilmorehill seen from the north east.

Anne Dick

Anne Dick

Right Glasgow University at sunset.
Below Finnieston Crane.

David Leslie

Anne Dick

Above Belmont Crescent. *Left* looking west down Great George Street.

Glasgow City Council

Private Collection

Above interior of the Kibble Palace.
Left the Stewart Fountain and Glasgow
University in the sunset painted by
Robert Eadie.

completed by J J Burnet, 1923-7, as a War Memorial, the chapel straddling it inside having much in common with his Barony Church (see p. 20).

Pearce Lodge, A G Thomson, 1887-8
As reward for his campaign against the destruction of the Old College, Thomson was given the gatehouse, which he composed of salvaged items: it includes the original coat-of-arms, twin balconies on heavy, carved corbels and the strapwork window heads, from the principal High Street façade. **Professors' Square,** built by G G Scott in the 1860s, is a stern, cavernous enclosure in Gothic-baronial, each home tall and narrow. No frills for the intellectually rigorous occupants.

John McIntyre Building, 1887 & 1895, J J Burnet
Livelier late Gothic, with a low tower, consciously Oxbridge in character. Originally designed to serve, firstly as the men, then women, students' union, it was superseded by buildings of the 1920s and 1960s respectively, and is now offices and bookshop. The **Botany and Engineering Buildings,** also by Burnet, 1900, were created in collaboration with John Oldrid Scott who was responsible for their squat external appearance. The **Natural Philosophy Buildings** by James Miller, 1905-6, are more picturesque neo-Jacobean. The 1958 **Engineering Building,** by Keppie Henderson & J L Gleave, is conservatively, brick-faced modern.

Zoology Building, 1923,
J J Burnet with Norman Dick
A playful pavilion: channelled stonework, and a projecting segmental-pedimented entrance tower balanced picturesquely by the ventilation cupola at the apex of the roof.

Chemistry Buildings, 1936-52,
T Harold Hughes, with D S R Waugh
An extremely distinguished complex of yellow banded brick, hinged by magnificent, semicircular, glazed, Mendelsohn-like stair towers which link the three wings of the building. The **Department of Natural Philosophy,** from 1957, by Basil Spence & Partners, is austerely rational: two long, horizontal, Portland stone floors, topped by a recessed fourth floor, standing upon a largely glazed ground floor. **Boyd-Orr Building,** University Avenue, 1972 by J L Gleave & Partners, is 11-storey group of towers of banded glass and concrete aggregate, linked by the liftshafts at the centre. The grey concrete-panelled protrusions are lecture theatres.

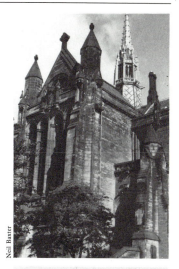

Neil Baxter

Neil Baxter

RCAHMS

Top University Chapel. *Middle* Zoology Building. *Above* one of the pair of splendid 1930s staircases joining the three wings of the Chemistry Building.

S

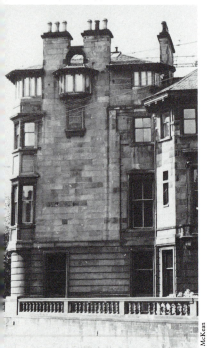

100 **Glasgow University Library**, Hillhead Street, 1968, William Whitfield
A product uniquely of its period. The architect aspired to soar on his magnificent hilltop site, complementary to the University. Turrets and spires being banned in the 1960s a soaring verticality is achieved by a cluster of thumbs—lift and service towers taken above the main bulk of the 11-storey Library.

101 **Hunterian Art Gallery**, 1972, William Whitfield
Elegant, toplit gallery with a magnificent collection of Whistlers, and Scots, Dutch and Realist paintings. Spaces are overtly modern, with ribbed bush-hammered concrete, polished wood, and plastered walls. Immense beaten aluminium doors, 1977, by Eduardo Paolozzi. The adjacent **Mackintosh House** is a reconstruction of the interiors of Charles and Margaret Mackintosh's second house, at 78 Southpark Avenue, and incorporates much furniture from their earlier one in Main Street, and from Windyhill. Do not be put off by the deep carpet and air-conditioning. This reconstruction allows us an enjoyment of the character of the different spaces and rooms, particularly the dark ground-floor dining-room and delicately white first-floor drawing room. The sight of the front door projecting within a concrete wall is an apt comment upon uncertainty—once compared to preserving the smile on the face of the Cheshire Cat after the animal had vanished.

Lilybank House, 1840
A small classical mansion with additions amended and extended by Alexander Thomson in 1869, now stranded on a little island flanked by the backs of numerous University departments. The impressive Ionic entrance portico and low south wing, with high-quality interiors, are by Thomson. Lilybank Gardens retains some red sandstone houses of c.1900.

Top Dining Room in the Mackintosh House, Hunterian Art Gallery. *Above* No 12 University Gardens. *Right* Modern Language Building.

12 University Gardens, 1900, J Gaff Gillespie
Splendid, idiosyncratic house; Glasgow Style freedom
blended with stone baroque, with some magnificent
interiors. Note the glazed turret. The remainder of
University Gardens was designed by J J Burnet with
exceptional interiors at **Nos 2, 4** and **14**.

Modern Languages Building, 1959, Walter Ramsay
Distinguished composition of 1930s plain precision:
raised ground floor, tall ground-floor windows, two
slimmer floors, above, a sculpture and an oversailing
cornice.

Queen Margaret Union,
1960, Walter Underwood & Partners
Somewhat transatlantic example of late 1960s
composition: plain arcade supporting two horizontally
proportioned floors above, with a visually projecting
top storey, jettied out.

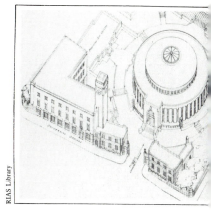

Original proposal for the Reading
Room, buildings and tower lining
University Avenue.

102 **Reading Room**, 1938-9,
T Harold Hughes and D S R Waugh
Centrepiece of a larger, unbuilt scheme in an axial
relationship with the University across the road,
focused upon a tall, clock-bearing tower. Its absence
explains the Reading Room's current lack of
architectural context. Like the Pantheon, it is circular
with a rectanglar entrance, but it is much lighter
inside: bright, galleried and graceful. The somewhat
Brutalist **Refectory,** behind, was designed in 1965
by Frank Fielden & Associates, recently humanised
into The Hub by Watson & Paterson.

103 **Wellington Church**, University Avenue,
1883-4, T L Watson
Crisp hillside classical temple with an extraordinarily
grand Corinthian-columned portico surmounting a
fine flight of steps (modelled on those of Wilkins'

Wellington Church.

187

University College, London) facing the University. The flanks of this otherwise pure box are enhanced by a colonnade of further large columns as a form of screen behind which the wall is set back so as to conceal the windows. Vast single-span galleried interior, concealed steel trusses behind a coffered ceiling, opulent woodwork.

Men's Union,
1928-9, John Arthur & Alan G McNaughtan
Time heals: when first built, the Union was thought heavy and reactionary: the dignity of its strong massing can now be better appreciated. A variant of crowstepped Scots with late traces of Glasgow Style, the design is focused upon the baronial, drum-towered entrance. The **Gilmorehill Church**, opposite, 1876-8, by James Sellars, now used as an examination hall, never received the full Normandy-Gothic spire which would have distinguished it.

Above Men's Union. *Right* Hillhead in the 1850s looking from Kelvin Bridge. Note the terraces of urban houses climbing the hillside creating a new suburb in the midst of countryside.

HILLHEAD
The steep hill bounded by Great Western Road, Byres Road and University Avenue developed almost as a new, grid iron hillside town overlooking countryside. The spine is Gibson Street, named after the proprietor James Gibson who bridged the Kelvin at Eldon Street in 1848; (the current bridge being iron Gothic tracery by Forman & McCall, 1895). Relatively grand dwellings to the east, terraces and tenements to north and west, it constitutes an unusual suburban survival with mature gardens and trees within this great city. As Gibson Street climbs upward, it is flanked by classical villas built on the original plots feued by the Gibsons and by later terraces.

Granby Terrace, 2-28 Hillhead Street, 1856, William Clarke
Grand classical terrace 47 bays long, with balustraded parapet. The architect, of Clarke & Bell, lived there himself. Note **Florentine House**, No 53 Hillhead Street—a pretty Georgian villa, c.1840.

94-106 Otago Street, 1874, Alexander Thomson
Four-storey building of strong horizontal emphasis,
lacking the decorative touches or classical references
for which Thomson was noted, but displaying
customary clarity of solid and void. Note also the
gracefully English red brick and white stone
Hubbard's Bakery, 1905, by Andrew Balfour with
its delicate tower and little Arts and Crafts oriel
windows. Note also the decaying, blue-painted,
Gothic barge-boarded, Gothic porched **farmhouse**
c.1860 abutting the later buildings.

41-53 Oakfield Avenue, 1865, Alexander Thomson
Recognisably Thomson. Framed by temple-like,
three-storey pavilions, this block consists of two-
storeyed houses with mansards and roof-lights.
Incised detail around the windows and customary
geometric precision in solid and void. **Nos 57-69**
comprise a fine terrace of 1868. **Nos 62-70** and
72-80 are further good classical terraces of 1855.

Southpark House, 64 Southpark Avenue, 1850
Handsome double villa, and the earliest in the street,
later developed as classical terraces viz **53-63**, 1867,
65-73, 1852, and the elongated **1-17**, 1862.

C McKean

RIAS Library

Hillhead High School, 1921-2, E G Wylie
Competition-winning design. An open-air school, on
a butterfly plan whose corridors are covered but open
to the air; designed to cleanse the city children of
any infectious disease by the icy blast. New plan is
matched by new materials: red brick and stone
detailing. Pleasant, swept-roofed Porter's Lodge.

Laurelbank School
Originally founded in the double villa of that name
built in 1842, the school now occupies Lilybank
Terrace and James Miller's 1893 red sandstone
Gothic **Belmont Parish Church**, in Great George
Street.

RIAS Library

Top detail from Oakfield Avenue by
Alexander Thomson. *Middle* E G
Wylie's competition-winning design for
Hillhead High School. *Above* section of
Belmont Church.

Top right D Y Cameron's sketch of Byres Road in 1894. *Above* glimpses of this busy area — *Top* Wilson's Bar, followed by the Salon Cinema, the Botanic Gardens garage, and typical tenement steps.

BYRES ROAD

The old route from Partick to the mansion of Byres of Partick (replaced by Athole Gardens). In 1851, Hugh MacDonald found '*nothing calling for a special remark*'. In 1872 it became the High Street of the Burgh of Hillhead with a fine Town Hall (demolished), and was lined with tenements, sometimes of considerable grandeur. Equally grand tenemental streets branch out on both sides: baronial red sandstone in Great George Street, plainer down toward Partick, and rippling wealth westwards to Horselethill. The northern end is now marked by modern buildings which, if nothing else, at least observe something close to the original scale.

105 **Curlers' Tavern**, 18th century
The oldest public house in the neighbourhood, on an even more ancient site, whose name derived from a curling pond opposite. Behind its shutters lies a solid, white two-storey stone building, with evenly spaced windows, wallhead chimney and plain detail. Murals inside feature celebrated customers including Hugh MacDiarmid. It acts as a reproach to the busy fussiness of the new, brick **Hillhead Underground Station**, 1980, which enfolds an existing cinema. Note **Wilson's Bar**, 1904, by William Reid: fine Glasgow Style windows whose designer was a minor master specialising in bars.

106 **Western Baths**, Cranworth Street, 1873, Clarke & Bell
Private club baths, only a hint of whose extravagantly Moorish interior appears in its Italian Gothic exterior. Wonderful carving, stained glass, marble, and double flight staircase within.

Hillhead Baptist Church, 1883, T L Watson
Son of Wellington Church translated into Greek Ionic and without the steps: short, tall church on a

corner site. **Electricity Sub-Station**, Vinicombe Street, is an attractive brick shed of 1912, tastefully fronted with semi-rusticated sandstone, with round-headed door and windows. Note also curious tenements with Gothic doors and windows uphill. The **Salon Cinema**, 1912-13, built by Brand & Lithgow, was built as the Hillhead Picture House, and is one of the few of that vintage which still retains its original purpose. Reticent for a cinema, its exterior is patterned with vague Glasgow Style decoration. The **Botanic Gardens Garage**, 1911, by D V Wyllie, one of the earliest in the city, is handsomely clad in green and cream tiles.

Top faintly Gothic tenement in Vinicombe Street. *Above* Kersland Street. *Top left* Curlers' Tavern. *Left* Western Baths, Cranworth Street.

Anne Dick

Mitchell Library

GREAT WESTERN ROAD

Toll route authorised by Act of Parliament in 1836, longest, straightest, and finest of Glasgow's thoroughfares, this broad and stylish boulevard has connected Cowcaddens with Anniesland and beyond since 1840. The original junction at St George's Cross is now compromised by a tangle of motorway slip roads.

107 **Clarendon Place**, 1839-41, Alexander Taylor
Taylor, who had worked in Edinburgh with Thomas Hamilton, planned a prestigious symmetrical development of *'first class houses, being in a healthful, well-aired, and rapidly improving situation'*, in twin blocks flanking the entrance to Maryhill Road. Each was to have a giant portico of four Tower of the Winds Corinthian columns, raised at first floor to form a grand gateway out of the city. The result was to have been not unlike Edinburgh's Waterloo Place. Only Clarendon Place was built. After much demolition, it has been given a brick bandage round its posterior, and just retains a proper urban scale and a good sense of proud elevation. It gives only a faint echo of what Taylor envisaged as one of *'the finest and most spacious approaches to the city'.*

The urban dignity of the route west is undiminished. Coherent two-tone tenements with banded stonework, through which wide leafy inlets intrude into Woodside, stretch as far as Kelvin Bridge channelling the views east and west.

108 **St Mary's Episcopal Cathedral**, 1871-84; spire 1893, Sir George Gilbert Scott & John Oldrid Scott
Originally built as a parish church from the proceeds of selling their Church in now unfashionable Renfield Street, Scott's Glasgow cathedral does not quite seem at ease. Its simple unfussed Early English Gothic has been given a restless patina of diaper work, rough stone and ashlar. Splendid landmark spire. Good Scott altar piece (in nave), Lorimer refurbishings, and Phoebe Traquair altarpiece, within elegant 13th-century arcading.

109 **Lansdowne Church**, 1861-2, John Honeyman
Where Scott failed, Honeyman, still a young man, had already succeeded. The spire, 218 ft high, is a key feature along the Great Western Road vista. It is immaculately slender with sculpted detail by William Mossman. The nave and transept eaves preserve the tenement scale, and a porched entrance gable faces west across the valley of the Kelvin: altogether *'perhaps the most attractive Victorian Gothic church in the city'.* It is T-plan in form, with a polygonal,

RCAHMS

Top Clarendon Place. *Middle* St Mary's Episcopal. *Above* Glasgow Academy.

vaulted apse. The aisles were designed as generous corridors from which individual doors opened through a partition to each of the pews for the well to do: lower orders were relegated upstairs.

> This Church is not for the poor and needy
> But for the rich and Dr Eadie,
> The rich step in and take their seat
> But the poor walk down to Cambridge Street.

Lansdowne Crescent, 1852, behind the Church is a curious late classical street leading to a polygon.

Great Western Bridge (Kelvin Bridge),
1890-1, Miller & Bell
The main spur to developments along Great Western Road was the predecessor of the present cast-iron bridge, with its Gothic tracery balustrade. Two previous, lower, bridges had crossed the river nearby, but this much larger structure consolidated Great Western Road as the most direct route west out of the city.

Glasgow Academy, 1878, H & D Barclay
Germanic institutional block: almost cubic in shape, an Ionic colonnade facing bands of recessed windows at first floor level. Original crispness ruined by continuous dormer window. Full height, top lit hall within. Good ironwork. The **War Memorial**, 1924, by A N Paterson.

10 **Caledonian Mansions**, 1897, James Miller
Neo-Jacobean frolic built as mansion flats, although first conceived as a small, up-market annexe to the

Above Lansdowne Church. *Below* Caledonian Mansions from the banks of the Kelvin. Note how much deeper the river runs than the level of Victorian Great Western Road.

Anne Dick

Central Hotel; reached by the new branch line from Central station to the new Kelvinbridge station. Exuberant turrets and carving; continuous, balustraded balcony on rear carried by huge corbels.

111 **Belmont Crescent,** 1870, John Honeyman
Crescent of tall, late classical terraced houses, set back behind their own gardens, sadly lacking both bookends through mining subsidence (a repeat of what happened 100 years earlier). Fine stair ironwork, plasterwork and fireplaces within. Belmont Street is lower in scale, but presents a fine sweep uphill to the Kelvin and the crown spire of the J J Stevenson's Stevenson Memorial Church, 1900-2. The Crescent is well restored: the street still waits. (Colour page 183).

Chimmy Chungas, 499 Great Western Road, 1886, R Duncan
Former grocery store, rather florid for this sedate location, now flats, offices and a restaurant. The corner is marked by an attenuated circular clock tower, complete with observation platform and a classical cupola. Note the Art Deco, terracotta former City Bakeries, opposite, by James Lindsay, 1929.

112 **Ruskin Terrace,** 1855-8
Originally St James Terrace, its eastern half rises like an Italian palazzo from a grand stair and ground floor with deeply recessed channel joints and Corinthian square pilasters. Enriched with pediments, balustrades and continuous cast-iron balconies above. The west part is much plainer. Sadly deteriorated.

Above former Coopers' store, with the former City Bakeries in the background. *Below* Muirhead Bone's view of Great Western Road looking east.

Hunterian Museum

Belgrave Terrace, 1856, Gildard & MacFarlane
Demure but elegant terrace of Italian inspiration, the central terrace houses being flanked by higher flatted end pavilions. Note the vermiculated (worm-eaten) keystones, rusticated pilasters, and open pedimented doorpiece facing Southpark Avenue.

Buckingham Terrace, 1852-8, J T Rochead
Particularly interesting classical-Italianate terrace, built in two portions, at the beginning and end of the decade: the eastern section very grand terrace houses, the western flatted. The canted bays, really oriel-windows carried upon a continuous consoled balcony, are amongst the earliest such in Glasgow. Details are very fine. Note the steady march of squarish attic windows beneath the cornice, and ranks of chimney stalks above; the stone balustrades to the front doors; and the way that the generous and well-lit entrances are recessed into the stone façade without any elaboration.

Above Buckingham Terrace. *Above left* Ruskin Terrace. *Left* North Park Terrace. *Below* the BBC.

13 **North Park Terrace**, Hamilton Drive, 1866, Alexander Thomson
Three-storey elevated terrace of regular proportion, with characteristic shallow-pilastered entrance porticos and spare Graeco-Egyptian detailing. The topmost storey appears as a line of pilasters running from end to end, and the principal windows on the first floor are linked by an intricately carved string-course of typical Thomson detail. Flanking it are the halves of an earlier, late classical terrace by Robert Crawford, 1857-9, lacking the subtlety of Thomson's work.

14 **BBC**, Queen Margaret Drive, 1869,
J T Rochead, completed by John Honeyman
Opulent Italianate palazzo, with a particularly fine frieze and elegant central hall. Built as a private Art Gallery for the Bell brothers (of ceramic fame) it became Queen Margaret College (the first Ladies' College in Scotland), before being bought by the

195

Above Charles Rennie Mackintosh's design for Queen Mary's College, now enfolded within the BBC.

BBC. Enfolded within the complex is the diminutive L-shaped Scots college, 1895, by John Keppie & Charles Rennie Mackintosh; visible only from the stairwell, but well worth the attempt. The BBC office was extended substantially in the 1930s by James Miller and again post-war.

115 **Bible Training Institute**, 731 Great Western Road, 1862, J J Stevenson
Diagonally opposite the entrance to the Botanic Gardens, the former Kelvinside Parish Church has an attenuated Italian Gothic pyramid spire (inspired by G E Street's churches in London). Its design was the earliest in Glasgow to show markedly foreign influences. Recent cleaning has highlighted the quality and subtle variations of its pale sandstone. Church complex is elegantly vertical. The interior has slim, cast-iron columned arcades, now divided at gallery level.

116 **Grosvenor Terrace**, 1855, J T Rochead
Stupendous, long, repetitive terrace: as though Rochead had cast a Venetian palace in iron and extruded it for a quarter mile. Three equal superimposed storeys, of huge round-headed windows provide a virtual curtain-wall of glass (necessary in this north-facing site) separated by the thinnest mullions of classical columns, Corinthian above Ionic above Doric in the normal way. The eastern portion was rebuilt after fire in the late 1970s, by T M Miller, using glass-reinforced concrete details, cast from the originals.

West of the Botanic Gardens, Great Western Road was laid out as a series of palatial terraces, to a plan by Decimus Burton, and became the height of fashion for high Victorian *haut-bourgeois* Glasgow: the epitome of carriage-trade living.

Below Bible Training Institute.
Below right Grosvenor Terrace.

D Walker

7 Kibble Palace, 1863, James Cousland
Magnificent glass cathedral bought from John Kibble at Coulport, and re-erected in the Botanics in 1871. Kibble retained free use of it for 21 years, using it for concerts and entertainment, and it became the social focus of the West End, the gentry crowding in for splendid events on summer evenings. Unfortunately, enthusiastic revellers damaged both the peace of the Botanics, and the plants themselves, and the Directors felt forced to buy out Kibble's lease. They became bankrupt in 1887, at which the City Corporation, the Society's main bond holder, took possession. An entrance 'aisle' and glazed 'transept' were added to the original from Coulport. Bleached white statues by Hamo Thornycroft, W Goscombe John etc were added, as well as a coffee area with pink and lime glazing (some of which—much faded—remain). The **Curator's House**, 1840, is by the prolific Charles Wilson. **Entrance Pavilions**, 1894, were built at the same time as the Botanic Gardens station, designed by James Miller. After the station's closure in 1939, its fantastic gilded domes attracted young people to the café which occupied part of the building. Gutted by fire in 1970, it was demolished.

The Kibble Palace. *Below* Great Western Road looking westwards in the 1890s. The Botanic Gardens lie on the right, and Grosvenor Terrace on the left. Anniesland, Bearsden and all places west lie in the haze beyond.

Botanic Gardens
Glasgow's first Botanic Garden was originally located on the High Street, as the Physic Garden of the University (see p 27). In 1815, a Botanic Garden Society was founded by a Mr Hopkirk of Dalbeath, subscribers were sought, and it was incorporated the following year, coincidentally with the appointment of Dr William Jackson as its first Professor of Botany, by Glasgow University. A small plot of land was bought near Charing Cross. In 1838, determined to profit from the rising land values caused by the development of Blythswood, it sold up, and bought a much larger plot on Great Western Road. By 1842 its garden was ready for its first visitors.

Mitchell Library

PICTORIAL GLOSSARY

1. Aedicule
2. Apron
3. Arcade
4. Arch
5. Architrave
6. Ashlar
7. Balustrade
8. Bow
9. Broken Pediment
10. Campanile
11. Capital
12. Cartouche
13. Cavetto
14. Channelled Stone
15. Column
16. Console
17. Corbel
18. Corbie-gabled
19. Cornice
20. Crowstepped
21. Curvilinear Gable
22. Cupola
23. Dome
24. Dormer
25. Drum
26. Eaves
27. Fanlight
28. Finial
29. Frieze
30. Glazing Bar
31. Keystone
32. Lancet
33. Loggia
34. Mullion
35. Niche
36. Palazzo
37. Pavilion Roof
38. Pediment
39. Pend
40. Piano Nobile
41. Pilaster/Pilastrade
42. Plinth
43. Portico
44. Quoin
45. Rotunda
46. Roundel
47. Screen Wall
48. Stack
49. Strapwork
50. String Course
51. Thermal Window
52. Tracery
53. Tripartite
54. Turnpike Stair
55. Tympanum
56. Venetian Window
57. Wallhead Gable

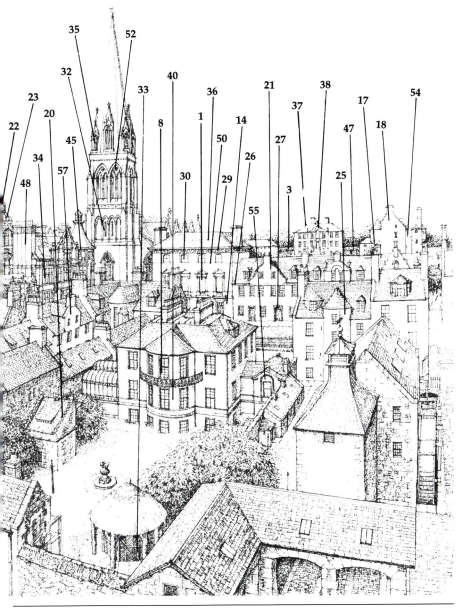

ACKNOWLEDGEMENTS

The authors are grateful to all those who have assisted them in this volume. They fall into three categories.

Special thanks are due to Anne Dick, of Building Pictures, who compiled a folio of outstanding photographs of Glasgow's architecture on our behalf; Ian Kinniburgh who prepared the map; Shona Adam who transformed David Walker's drawing into the illustrated glossary; the Royal Commission on the Ancient and Historical Monuments of Scotland for its genially helpful response to an exceptional demand for photographs, Douglas Macgregor for some of his beautiful colour photographs, White House Studios, Antony Alexander for two of his paintings, Duncan McAra for putting up with us, Dorothy (Lena) Smith for typing and retyping the manuscripts, and Margaret Wilson for administration.

The British Architectural Library, the Trustees of the Sir John Soane Museum, the Hunterian Art Gallery the University of Glasgow, Historic Buildings and Monuments SDD, the National Trust for Scotland, the Mitchell Library, Glasgow Museums and Art Galleries, the Property Services Agency, RIAS Library and Drawings Collection, and the National Galleries of Scotland all kindly gave us permission to reproduce some of their treasures. Sources of illustrations are noted against each.

Great assistance in the compilation of this volume was given by the following: AHAUS Archive of the Department of Architecture and Building Science—University of Strathclyde, Judith Anderson, ASSIST, Patricia Bascomb, Neil Baxter, Simon Berry, Boswell Mitchell & Johnston, Harry Bunch of Hurd Rolland & Partners, Bob Burnett, Ian Campbell, I Stuart Campbell, Brian Carter of Arup Associates, City of Glasgow Planning Department, Robert Clow, Philip Cocker & Partners, Comprehensive Design, James Cunning Young and Partners, Joyce Deans, Archie Doak, Michael Donnelly, Andrew Doolan of Kantel (Edinburgh) plc, Elder & Cannon, Joe Fisher and his helpful staff in the Glasgow Room of the Mitchell Library, John Forgie, Ian Fraser, Tony Gorzkowski, Ian Gow, Stuart Gulliver, Historic Buildings & Monuments, Dr Martin Hopkinson, George Horspool, John R Hume, Robert Inglis of the Royal Scottish Academy of Music and Drama, G R M Kennedy & Partners, Keppie Henderson, Elspeth King, David Leslie, Mackay & Forrester, Aognhus MacKechnie, Ranald MacInnes, Hugh McAndrew, Frank McConnell, John Maule McKean, Richard McKean, McGurn Logan Duncan & Opfer, McMenan & Brown, Findlay McQuarrie, Hugh Martin Partnership, Matheson Gleave, Dr Deborah Mays, R S G Nicol, Bill Nimmo, Jack Notman, Raymond O'Donnell, Page & Park, Parr Partnership, PSA, Jim Rennie, Anne Riches, Peter Robinson, Scott Brownrigg & Turner, SDA, Ronald Sheridan, Fiona Sinclair, John Sinclair of the Royal Faculty of Procurators, Strathclyde Regional Archives, Robin Th'ng, Mark Watson, Watson Salmond & Gray, Sir Alwyn Williams, Elizabeth Williamson, Wylie Shanks.

REFERENCES

The arrangement of this guide precludes the normal methods of reference. The following list includes the principal sources which have been used in this publication.

ANDERSON, JAMES **Provosts of Glasgow**; ANNAND, LOUISE **A Glasgow Sketch Book; Architect, The; Biographical Sketches of the Lord Provosts of Glasgow 1833-1883;** BOLITHO WILLIAM **Cancer of the Empire;** BONE MUIRHEAD **Glasgow—50 drawings; Book of Glasgow** Civic and Empire Week; **Book of the Bishop's Castle;** BOWMAN W DODGSON **Glasgow and the Clyde;** BROTCHIE T C F **Glasgow rivers and streams;** BROTCHIE T C F **Some sylvan scenes near Glasgow; Builder, The; Building Years; Building Industries; Building News;** CAMPBELL WILLIAM **History of the Incorporation of Cordiners; Chronicles of Gotham;** CLELAND JAMES **Annals of Glasgow;** COCHRANE HUGH **Impressions of Glasgow;** COWAN, JAMES **From Glasgow's Treasure Chest;** CULLEN AND SCOTT **Views of Glasgow** 1834; DAICHES DAVID **Glasgow; Dean of Guild Records;**

DENHOLM JAMES History of the City of Glasgow 1798;
DOAK ARCHIE ed. Glasgow at a glance; DUNCAN RICHARD
Notices and documents—Literary History of Glasgow; EADIE
ROBERT Glimpses of Glasgow; EYRE-TODD GEORGE The
Book of Glasgow Cathedral; EYRE-TODD GEORGE History
of Glasgow; FAIRBAIRN THOMAS Relics of Ancient
architecture of Glasgow; FRAZER DANIEL The Making of
Buchanan Street; Glasgow Advertiser; Glasgow Herald;
GOMME ANDOR AND DAVID WALKER The architecture of
Glasgow; ed. J S F GORDON; Glasghu Facies; Glasgow, A
Connoisseur's Guide; Glasgow Ancient and Modern;
HANLEY CLIFF Dancing in the Streets; Skinful of Scotch;
HONEYMAN, JOHN The age of Glasgow Cathedral; JONES
Directory of Glasgow 1787; KILPATRICK JAMES Literary
Landmarks of Glasgow; KINCHIN JULIET AND PERILLA
Glasgow's Great Exhibitions; KING JESSIE Glasgow City of
the West; LANG J MARSHALL Glasgow and the barony
thereof; LEE JOHN K Greyfriars, Glasgow; LEIGHTON AND
SWAN Views on the Clyde 1830; LEIGHTON AND JOSEPH
SWAN Views of Glasgow and environs 1828; LINDSAY
MAURICE Portrait of Glasgow; Lord Provosts of Glasgow;
LUGTON THOMAS The Old ludgings of Glasgow; LUGTON
THOMAS The story of Glasgow Cathedral; LUMSDEN AND
AITKEN History of the Hammermen of Glasgow;
MACDONALD, HUGH Rambles round Glasgow; McDOWALL
J K People's History of Glasgow; MACGEORGE ANDREW
Old Glasgow; MACLEHOSE; Memoirs and portraits of one
hundred Glasgow Men; MACLELLAN ARCHIBALD Essay on
Cathedral Church; MACKENZIE PETER Old reminiscences
of Glasgow; McURE JOHN History of Glasgow; MALLOCH
MACLEOD Book of Glasgow Anecdote; Merchant's House, A
View Of; Midnight Scenes; MITCHELL J OSWALD Old
Glasgow Essays; MUIR JAMES Glasgow streets and places;
MURRAY, DAVID Memories of the Old College of Glasgow;
OAKLEY CHARLES The Second City; NAPIER James Notes
and reminiscences of Partick; Old Country Houses of the Old
Glasgow Gentry; OLD GLASGOW CLUB 75 anniversary;
PAGAN JAMES History of Glasgow and the Cathedral;
PAGAN JAMES Glasgow Past and present; PHIPPS ELVIRA
Memorials of Clutha; Prospect; RENWICK ROBERT Glasgow
Memorials; Scottish Building Chronicle; SENEX and JAMES
PAGAN Glasgow Past and Present; SIMPSON WILLIAM
Glasgow in the 40s; SMALL DAVID Bygone Glasgow; SMALL
DAVID Quaint bits of old Glasgow in 1885; SMART AILEEN
Villages of Glasgow; STEWART GEORGE Curiosities of
Glasgow Citizenship; STEWART GEORGE Progress of
Glasgow; STOTHERS THOMAS Glasgow, Renfrewshire and
Lanarkshire New Year Album; STRANG Dr JOHN Glasgow
and its clubs; Necropolis Glasguensis; STUART ROBERT
Views and notices of Glasgow in former times 1848;
University of Glasgow through 5 centuries; URIE JOHN;
Reminiscences of eighty years; WALLACE ANDREW History
of Glasgow; WHITE JAMES Foundations of Glasgow;
WORSDALL FRANK Victorian City.

INDEX

ARCHITECTURAL
GUIDES
TO SCOTLAND

The acclaimed RIAS/Landmark series of Architectural Guides to Scotland is essential reading for people interested in the built history of the country.

SERIES EDITOR: CHARLES McKEAN

Already Published

EDINBURGH: by Charles McKean. Now in its 3rd edition.

DUNDEE: by Charles McKean and David Walker.
Now in its 2nd edition.

STIRLING AND THE TROSSACHS: by Charles McKean 1985.

ABERDEEN: by W. A. Brogden 1986.
Now in its 2nd edition.

THE SOUTH CLYDE ESTUARY: by Frank Arneil Walker 1986.

CLACKMANNAN: by Adam Swan 1987.

THE DISTRICT OF MORAY: by Charles McKean 1987.

Forthcoming

FIFE: BANFF AND BUCHAN: NORTH CLYDE ESTUARY: BORDERS AND BERWICK: SHETLAND: CENTRAL SCOTLAND: NORTH HIGHLANDS

The series is winner of the *Glenfiddich Living Scotland Award* 1985.

These and other RIAS books: and books on Scottish architecture are all available from the RIAS Bookshop, 15 Rutland Square, Edinburgh EH1 2BE.
031-229 7205.

Also available:

The SCOTTISH THIRTIES: by Charles McKean. An explanation of Scotland and its architecture in the years 1930-40. 1987.

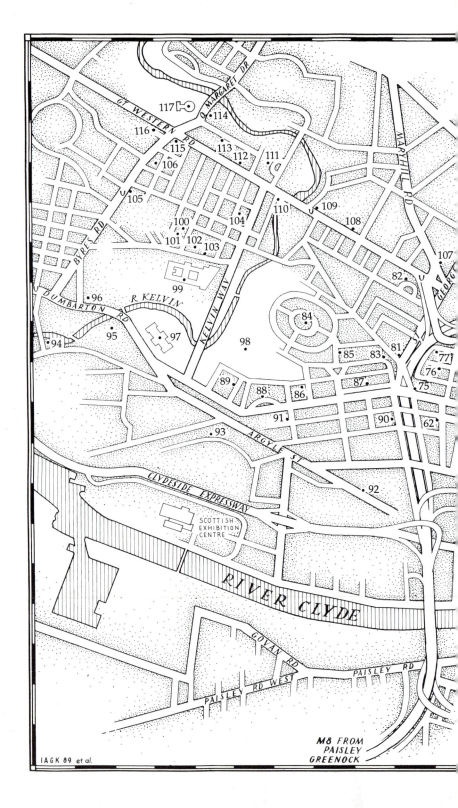